Armed for
SPIRITUAL WARFARE
WORKBOOK

JAMIE BUCKINGHAM

A master story-teller, Jamie Buckingham has delighted millions — in person and in print. He has written more than 40 books, including biographies of Nicky Cruz *(Run, Baby, Run)*, Pat Robertson *(Shout it from the Housetops)*, Corrie Ten Boom *(Tramp for the Lord)* and Kathryn Kuhlman *(Daughter of Destiny)*. He is an award-winning columnist for *Charisma* magazine and is Editor-in-Chief of *Ministries Today*.

One of America's foremost authorities on the Sinai, in recent years he has written and produced a number of video teaching tapes on location in Israel.

He holds graduate degrees in English literature and theology. A distinguished Bible teacher, he is popular among Roman Catholics, Episcopalians, evangelicals and Pentecostals. He is founder and senior pastor of the Tabernacle Church, an inter-denominational church in Melbourne, Florida, where he has served 24 years. He lives on rural property on Florida's east coast, with his wife, Jackie, surrounded by five married children and 12 grandchildren.

Armed for

SPIRITUAL WARFARE

WORKBOOK

by Jamie Buckingham

To be used with "Armed for Spiritual Warfare"
Video Tape Series

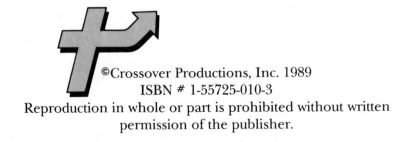

CONTENTS

Armed for
SPIRITUAL WARFARE

INTRODUCTION

Christians are under attack from a deadly but invisible enemy. God has given us orders to be armed for battle in spiritual warfare.

As we finish the countdown on the second millennium since the birth of Jesus and prepare to enter the next—and what many believe to be the final—phase of history, Satan is mounting a massive attack against Christians and the church. As a result there is a great resurgence of interest in spiritual warfare. Christians of all persuasions are realizing they do not have to be pushed around by the devil. Jesus Christ has given us authority—not only to cast out demons, but to bash in the gates of hell.

Several years ago, believing it was time to use video tape to communicate spiritual truth, I took a camera crew into the Sinai desert. Following the footsteps of Moses I video-taped brief messages at various locations. I combined this with a Bible study workbook and called the series *The Journey to Spiritual Maturity*. Shortly after that material was distributed I began getting letters from prison and jail chaplains—as well as Bible study leaders—who were working with men and women behind bars. They said the material was ideal for prison Bible studies since it combined the visual (video) with the written (workbook) with an instructor. Video alone is not suffcient to convey truth. It must be combined with the personal touch of a teacher to answer—and ask—questions, and a workbook to stimulate actual Bible reading and study.

Chuck Colson's Prison Fellowship organization asked us to prepare three more series using the same technique. These would be used in all their prison Bible studies. I returned to Israel and produced—on location—*Ten Parables of Jesus, Ten Miracles of Jesus*, and *Ten Bible People Like Me.*

As these were being distributed in the prisons it became evident that they were also ideal for small group Bible studies in homes and churches—as well as for individuals wishing to study the scripture in the privacy of their own home. As a result tens of thousands of these tapes are now in circulation all over America.

It was then I decided to take on the big project—*Spiritual Warfare*. Video segments 1-3 and 10 were filmed on location in Israel. Segments 4-9 were done in a studio at the Community of Jesus on Cape Cod, Massachusetts, with the assistance of "Ivan the Ironman"—a piece of medieval armor I used on the set to illustrate putting on the "full armor of God." From the moment

I began the project until I finished I was under constant attack from Satan. I quickly realized as long as I only theorized about spiritual warfare Satan didn't care. But when I began teaching, and preparing materials that would arm others for battle, he mounted an all-out attack against me, against my mind, against my equipment (my word processor in particular), and against my loved ones. I was forced—as a matter of survival—to practice what I was preaching. I can testify, from personal experience, to the methods of spiritual warfare I cover in this study.

Before you get started, spend time praying. Continue to pray as you study. Let God dispatch His angels to protect you. You will soon realize the battle belongs to God. The victory in spiritual warfare is already ours because of what Jesus has done at Calvary. Now claim it—and stand victorious!

Jamie Buckingham
Melbourne, Florida

GETTING THE MOST FROM THIS STUDY

Using the accompanying video tape, this workbook is designed to lead you, step by step, into an understanding of spiritual warfare. You will learn what spiritual warfare is. Who the enemy is (Satan and his demons). Who our allies are in the battle (angels). And, by studying the Bible, how to arm yourself so you will not only be safe in the battle—but emerge triumphant. The video segments of these lessons are the "pictures" for the book. They are designed to help you visualize what you are studying. The video can be viewed separately—much as a person might "read" *National Geographic* magazine by simply looking at the pictures and captions and not reading the accompanying articles. However, to get the full impact of the study you need to look at the video, then, using this workbook, study the Bible verse by verse.

The material on the video tape and in this workbook can be used in a number of ways. It can be the basis of an individual study. It may be used in a small group, such as a Bible study group, a Sunday school class, or a house group. Experience has shown the greatest benefit comes when a group of people study the material together under a leader who is well-prepared on the subject.

HELPS FOR THE LEADER

The group leader or teacher preparing to take a group of people into a study of Spiritual Warfare needs to give attention to the following:

I. NECESSARY MATERIALS

* A good color television set with a screen large enough

* A reliable video player.

* A power source within reach of the plugs for the TV and VCR.

* Comfortable seating so each person may see the TV screen and the teacher.

* A Bible for each student. The workbook uses scripture quotes from the New International Version (NIV), but any Bible will do.

* A workbook for each student.

* Pen or pencil for each student.

2. Preparation

Before teaching others you should not only view the entire video series—all 10 segments—but you should work your way through this workbook. You will find a number of scripture references. Study them in depth before attempting to lead the class in discussion. You are not expected to have all the answers. Your job will be to help the students ask the right questions and stimulate them to explore the Bible for themselves.

3. Be Aware

Satan knows the kind of power that is generated when a group of people get together to study spiritual warfare. He will, invariably, strike back. Be aware of his intent before you begin the study. Never begin a study of spiritual warfare without making sure you are "dressed in the full armor of God." Do not enter this study casually or with self-confidence. To do so means you are running the risk suffered by the seven sons of Sceva in Acts 19 who tried to cast out demons without spiritual authority. The demons stripped off their clothes and battered their bodies until they had to flee for their lives. It is imperative you open each class session by placing yourself and your class under the blood and authority of Jesus. To do less invites disaster, for Satan and his demons will do everything possible to keep you from completing the study.

As you lead the class be aware that each person present is going through some kind of crisis in his or her life which calls for spiritual warfare. This could be a financial crisis, a grief experience, a problem with personal identification, a battle with demons or temptation, a crisis in the home, spiritual confusion, or a number of different mountains which seem too high to climb and too thick to tunnel through. Your awareness of their need will help when it comes to answering questions and leading discussion. Do not be afraid to pause at any place in the discussion and minister to that person or persons—laying aside the study and entering into literal warfare in behalf of the person in need.

4. Stick to the Subject

Your job, as teacher, is to hold the discussion to spiritual warfare. Satan will do everything in his power to cause someone in the class to try to lead you on some rabbit chase down a side path. Others will try to monopolize the discussion. Some will try to entice you into an argument over some minor point. It is important you stick, as nearly as possible, to the outline of the subject at hand. The material has been carefully designed to build principle on principle with the eventual aim of the student becoming "thoroughly equipped for every good work" (II Timothy 3:17). Do not preach. Do not monopolize the conversation yourself. Do not allow the class to drift from the subject matter.

5. Stimulate Discussion

Remember, your job as teacher is not to give answers—even if you know them—but to skillfully stimulate discussion and encourage each student to find God's Word for his own life. The Holy Spirit will help you, for He wants each one to learn firsthand the principles of spiritual warfare—and to apply them to his life. Do not limit yourself to the material covered in this workbook.

It is merely a guide, a primer for discussion. Allow the Holy Spirit to direct your class sessions.

6. Be Sensitive to Time

If your class has more than an hour for each study, arrange for a break of a few minutes for refreshment or a stretch. If the group discussion is dynamic, or if someone in the class indicates a need for personal ministry, you may want to keep the session going. Or, if the particular subject is stimulating extra discussion, you may want to put off the next segment in order to continue that one for an additional week. If that is the case, I recommend the class review the same video segment at the opening of the second week of study to stimulate discussion.

Remember, just because the class has ended does not mean the Holy Spirit's work is over. In fact, in all probability the greatest work of the Spirit in the lives of the students will take place after the class is over. That means you may want to open the next class with a brief report on the Spirit's activity in the area of spiritual warfare since the class last met. Each workbook chapter closes with a "practical exercise" which is designed to stimulate activity during the week and calls for reports at the next session.

Helps for Students

Before you start this course ask yourself these questions:

* Am I really committed to living a victorious life in Christ?

* Am I willing to commit myself to attending all the sessions of this course unless unavoidably detained?

* Am I willing to open my mind to new truth beyond what I now believe?

* Am I willing to prepare ahead of time through prayer and by reading my Bible and doing all the work in my workbook?

* Am I willing to enter into the group discussion—asking questions and expressing my personal opinions?

* Am I willing, if I know God is prodding me, to ask for and receive personal ministry from the group or someone in the group?

* Am I willing to enter into spiritual warfare on behalf of myself and others?

If you answered "no" to any of these questions you may want to reconsider whether you should take this course. In this course you will "handle the Word of God." You will find yourself in face-to-face confrontations with Satan and his demons. You will be called on to intercede for others who are under attack. You should not enter into this course lightly or unadvisedly. Once you begin a serious study of spiritual warfare, you will be dealing with the supernatural area of life. If you stick to the Word of God, however, claim the blood of Jesus, receive the filling of the Holy Spirit, and dress yourself in the full armor of God, you will always be victorious. If you are not ready for that to happen, you may want to sit this one out.

On the other hand, if you answered "yes" to the questions, you're ready to proceed. Here are some immediate steps you can take to insure maximum benefit from the course.

I. SET GOALS

This course is designed to help you understand not only the nature of spiritual warfare, but the nature of God, angels, Satan and demons. It does not matter whether you are young or old, a seasoned Christian or just a seeker—you can be victorious over the devil. Like the rain, which falls on the just and the unjust, victory is for all who call on the name of the Lord. The principles learned over these next several class sessions will help you be triumphant in battle. What are your needs? What kind of spiritual attacks are you going through? Are you tired of giving in to temptation, of having things always go wrong, of sickness and despair? Set goals and let this study help you get there.

2. HONESTLY EVALUATE YOUR PRESENT CONDITION

What are your needs—your real needs? Honestly evaluate your present condition as you begin this study of spiritual warfare, for without a willingness to face yourself it will be extremely difficult to understand what God is saying to you concerning your past, present, and future.

The commitment to dig into the Bible must be accompanied by constant self-measurement and self-inventory. You know the kind of person you already are. You know the level of commitment you already display. You know your faith level. The question you must now face is: Am I willing to take my stand against the devil and let God work through me in spiritual warfare?

At the end of each chapter there is a place where you—in the privacy of your own study—can evaluate your personal progress. The answers you give to the questions will give you a spitiual indicator of your progress week by week. The questions will also help fix the Word of God more firmly in your heart and thus provide a reservoir of truth that the Holy Spirit can draw upon in the training and reshaping of your life until you are conformed to the image of Jesus.

3. YOU'LL NOT PASS THIS WAY AGAIN

Although God gives each man and woman infinite chance to improve and move into spiritual maturity, there are certain times in battle when you must strike and strike quickly. Thus, when discussion in class opens the door for you to express yourself, ask for prayer or take authority over a demon, do not hesitate to respond. One of the things you will be doing during these sessions will be learning to hear God—just as Jesus did. When Jesus confronted Satan on the Mount of Temptation He answered each charge Satan threw at Him with the Word of God. Satan, the Bible says, was forced to pull back and slink away. He returned, many times, but each time Jesus sent him away with a single rebuke. You, too, have that authority. But it is authority which must be taken.

As you enter into this study of spiritual warfare you will often hear God as He gives you direction. If you do what He tells you to do, regardless of how illogical lt may seem at the time, you will experience wonderful victory.

4. STUDY EACH CHAPTER BEFORE CLASS

Ideally, you should study each chapter in this workbook before coming to class. Look up each Scripture reference, answer all the questions by filling in the blanks and circling the true/false answers. Of course, if it is impossible to study ahead of time, you should still take part in the class activities.

5. Set Your Own Pace

One of the lessons you will learn as you study the Bible is this: God's patience is infinite as long as you are moving toward Him. The only time you will begin to feel pressure is when you close your mind, dig in your heels, or get off God's trail by pursuing false ideas and concepts. Do not be afraid to move slowly. To rush through this study may mean you learn all the right religious answers, but miss the Holy Spirit, who is the one who leads you safely through the mine fields of spiritual warfare. This course is designed to provoke you to do your own searching, thinking, and praying—and to personally take authority over demons—that you may see concrete results from your faith in God.

6. Check Your Progress

If you are taking this study as part of a group, once you have completed the course, ask your group leader to sit down with you and review where you are in life. Remember the question Jesus asked the man at the pool of Bethesda: "Do you really want to be healed?" A lot of people want to have victory over Satan but are not sure they want to pay the cost.

7. Finally

Each chapter has a number of questions with accompanying Scripture references. By looking up the references you should be able to answer all the questions. Do not be afraid to fill in the blanks—even if you give the wrong answers. No one is going to grade you. This course is like those wonderful Special Olympics for handicapped children—everyone who enters is called a winner, regardless of how he finishes.

You will be awarded a Certificate of Completion at the end of the course, signed by me and your instructor. All you have to do is finish. That makes you a winner. By looking up the answers you will learn. Go ahead, try it. It's fun to venture out—especially when God goes with you.

And remember, the only thing more exciting than studying the truth about spiritual warfare is realizing that as you pray and take your stand against the devil, God will make you victorious.

Jamie Buckingham

Unless otherwise stated, Scripture quotations are taken from the New International Version (NIV) of the Bible, copyright 1978 by New York International Bible Society and published by Zondervan Corporation, Grand Rapids, Michigan. Used by permission.

LESSON 1
PRINCIPLES OF
SPIRITUAL WARFARE
VIDEO REFERENCE: #1

1. INTRODUCTION

The greatest battle of all history was not fought between flesh and blood, between opposing armies or armed warriors. It was a battle in the spirit realm between the two most powerful forces in the universe—the Source of Evil, known in the Bible as Satan, and the Commander in Chief of the Lord's host, the Son of God. Even though the battle was won by Jesus Christ, the skirmishes continue to this day. On one side is Satan with his countless demons. On the other side are Jesus and His angels. The battle is for the bodies and souls of men and women on earth. This battle is called spiritual warfare.

2. JESUS' BAPTISM

APPROXIMATELY HOW OLD WAS JESUS WHEN HE BEGAN HIS PUBLIC MINISTRY? (Luke 3:23).

_____ 24

_____ 30

_____ 45

_____ 60

WHAT EVENT MARKED THE INAUGURATION OF HIS MINISTRY? (Luke 3:21-22).

_____

WHAT HAPPENED AS JESUS WAS BEING BAPTIZED? (Luke 3:22).

_____

_____

WHAT DID GOD SAY TO JESUS AT HIS BAPTISM? (Luke 3:22).

_____

_____

HOW DOES LUKE DESCRIBE JESUS FOLLOWING HIS BAPTISM? (Luke 4:1).

_____

Jesus had been empowered—filled with the Holy Spirit—and was ready to begin His ministry of teaching and miracles. But first the Holy Spirit led Him into the Judean Wilderness to fast and pray. It was here the Son of God came face to face with Satan.

Satan had carefully planned his attack against Jesus, hoping to derail the Son of God before His ministry got off the ground. He presented Jesus with three temptations—one aimed at each of the three elements that were going to be strengths of Jesus' work on earth.

The devil does that—goes after a person in the areas in which he is strong. There's little use in going after weak areas—they don't pose a threat.

3. THE FIRST TEMPTATION

DID SATAN TRY TO TEMPT JESUS BEFORE OR AFTER JESUS HAD BEEN FILLED WITH THE HOLY SPIRIT? (Luke 4:1-2).

_____ before

_____ after

HOW LONG HAD JESUS BEEN IN THE WILDERNESS WITHOUT FOOD OR WATER WHEN SATAN APPROACHED HIM? (Luke 4:1-2).

_____ Seven times

_____ a few hours

_____ two weeks

_____ 40 days

_____ a year and a half

WHAT WAS SATAN'S FIRST TEMPTATION? (Luke 4:3).

_____

_____

WHAT WAS JESUS' RESPONSE? (Luke 4:4).

_____

_____

_____

LOOK UP THE OLD TESTAMENT REFERENCE AND WRITE IT HERE:

DEUTERONOMY 8:3: _____

_____

_____

WHAT DO YOU THINK WAS THE SIGNIFICANCE OF THIS TEMPTATION?

_____

_____

_____

MATTHEW 14:13-21 RECORDS ONE OF JESUS' GREATEST MIRACLES. WHAT WAS IT?

_____

_____

By tempting Jesus to turn the rocks into bread, Satan was encouraging Jesus to fill not only His own stomach, but to feed all the other starving people in the world, thereby setting up a kingdom based on materialism and good works.

In His time on earth, Jesus *did* feed the hungry. However, He knew that filling a person's stomach was not the goal of His ministry.

WHAT "FOOD" DID JESUS SAY WE SHOULD WORK FOR? (John 6:27)

_____

_____

WHAT IS THE "BREAD OF LIFE"? (John 6:35) _____

HOW IS THE "BREAD OF LIFE" DIFFERENT FROM OUR REGULAR FOOD? (John 6:35)

_____

_____

4. The Second Temptation

What was Satan's second temptation? (Luke 4:5-7).

_____

_____

What was Jesus' response? (Luke 4:8).

_____

_____

_____

Look up the Old Testament reference and write it here:
Deuteronomy 6:13: _____

_____

_____

_____

What do you think was the significance of this temptation?

_____

_____

_____

_____

What authority did Jesus know God had given Him? (Matthew 28:18)

_____

_____

Throughout His ministry, Jesus displayed complete authority over the things of the earth—the laws of physics, demons, even over death itself. He refused to be tempted by the false sense of power Satan was offering Him.

5. The Third Temptation

What was Satan's third temptation? (Luke 4:9-11).

_____

_____

What was Jesus' response? (Luke 4:12).

_____

LOOK UP THE OLD TESTAMENT REFERENCE AND WRITE IT HERE:

Deuteronomy 6:16: _____

_____

_____

WHAT DO YOU THINK WAS THE SIGNIFICANCE OF THIS TEMPTATION?

_____

_____

_____

WHO DID SATAN SAY WOULD COME TO JESUS' RESCUE? (Luke 4:10-11).

_____

WHO CAME TO MINISTER TO JESUS AFTER SATAN LEFT? (Matthew 4:11).

_____

The angels were available at any time to come to Jesus' aid. But Jesus resisted the temptation to build a kingdom based on magic and presumption. At many points in His ministry, Jesus, in faith, asked things of God. But He knew there was a wide difference between faith and presumption. Faith is believing what God says is true. Presumption is going beyond what God says and testing Him—trying to make Him do what you want Him to do. Jesus would have none of that.

WHAT DID JESUS' THREE RESPONSES HAVE IN COMMON?

_____

WAS JESUS THE ONLY ONE WHO KNEW THE SCRIPTURES?

_____

LOOK UP THE OLD TESTAMENT REFERENCE USED BY SATAN AND WRITE IT HERE: PSALM 91:11-12:

_____

_____

_____

_____

WHAT DID SATAN DECIDE TO DO AFTER HIS DEFEAT IN THE WILDERNESS? (Luke 4:13).

_____ graciously accept defeat

_____ check Jesus' Scripture references

_____ leave Jesus until an opportune time

6. DRESSING FOR SUCCESS

The Bible teaches that as followers of Christ, we are involved in a spiritual battle. Just as Jesus was tempted by Satan, we, too, can expect to be attacked—often in the areas of our greatest strengths, or in those areas God wants to use for ministry. The apostle Paul, writing to the new believers in the city of Ephesus, closes his letter with instructions on how to prepare for spiritual warfare—how to "dress for success" in the battle against Satan and his demons.

WHAT DOES PAUL TELL THE EPHESIANS TO PUT ON? (Ephesians 6:11)

_____

WHY SHOULD THEY PUT ON THE ARMOR? (Ephesians 6:11 & 13)

_____

_____

_____

_____

LIST THE COMPONENTS OF GOD'S ARMOR: (Ephesians 6:14-17)

1. _____
2. _____
   _____
3. _____
4. _____
5. _____
6. _____

Obviously, Paul is not talking about putting on physical armor—articles that can be retrieved from the closet, pulled onto our bodies, and secured with buckles and straps. Nevertheless, we need to "put on" our spiritual armor, just as the Bible teaches that we are to "put on Christ"—by faith, taking on His very nature.

That's how we're to put on the full armor of God: by faith. To do this, I've found it can sometimes be helpful to "act it out." I want to challenge you, over the course of time you have committed to this Bible study, to do something that I do every morning as I get dressed. As I reach for my pants and belt, I say, "I am putting on the belt of truth." As I reach for my shirt, I say, "I am putting on the breastplate of righteousness." As I put on my shoes, I say, "My feet are fitted with the readiness that comes from the gospel of peace." Then, continuing to speak out aloud, I take up my shield of faith, put the helmet of salvation over my head, and take a few swings with my sword of the Spirit.

Silly? I'm sure it sounds that way. But I guarantee that if you do this consistently—especially as we learn more about each piece of armor in upcoming lessons—you will quickly begin to understand the value of preparing yourself for battle by daily putting on the full armor of God.

7. WRAP UP

In his first major battle with Satan, Jesus emerged victorious. We, too, can be victorious in spiritual warfare. The weapons Jesus had available on the Mount of Temptation—both offensive and defensive—are also available to us today. We will learn more about what they are and how to use them in upcoming lessons.

8. FINAL LESSON

If we are in Jesus, the ultimate victory over Satan is always ours.

9. PERSONAL REVIEW QUESTIONS

Circle T (true) or F (false)

1. T F After his baptism, Jesus immediately began to minister to the people.

2. T F Once you are filled with the Spirit, Satan must withdraw and leave you alone.

3. T F Satan tends to attack a person in his weak areas.

4. T F It's okay to presume that God will do what you want Him to do; that's what the Bible calls "faith."

5.　T　　F　　Jesus always combated Satan's temptations by quoting the Scriptures.

6.　T　　F　　Satan can twist the Bible for his own purposes.

7.　T　　F　　All authority in heaven and on earth has been given to Jesus.

8.　T　　F　　Angels ministered to Jesus in the wilderness.

9.　T　　F　　After his defeat in the wilderness, Satan knew better than to try to battle Jesus again.

10.　T　　F　　We cannot defeat Satan the way Jesus did because we do not have the same resources available to us.

10. MEMORY VERSE

Ephesians 6:10 (Memorize, then write it on these lines.)

_____

_____

_____

Over the next several weeks our goal is to memorize Ephesians 6:10-18, the Bible's definitive guideline for waging spiritual warfare. After each succeeding lesson, we will add an additional verse until we have memorized the entire passage.

11. PRACTICAL EXERCISE

This week note the ways Satan tempts *you* in the three areas he tempted Jesus.

RECALL HOW YOU RESPOND.

1. PULLING YOU AWAY FROM THE *BEST* BY TEMPTING YOU TO DO SOMETHING *GOOD* INSTEAD:

_____

_____

_____

_____

_____

2. TEMPTING YOU TO MISUSE YOUR SPIRITUAL AUTHORITY

_____

_____

_____

_____

_____

3. TEMPTING YOU TO PRESUME ON GOD:

_____

_____

_____

_____

_____

_____

TRUE OR FALSE ANSWERS:

1-F, 2-F, 3-F, 4-F, 5-T, 6-T, 7-T, 8-T, 9-T, 10-F

NOTES

LESSON 2
SATAN AND HIS DEMONS
VIDEO REFERENCE: #2

1. INTRODUCTION

Every soldier knows that the first rule of warfare is to identify your enemy. If you do not know who your enemy is, what kind of strength he possesses, and what his tactics are, your hope of victory is greatly reduced.

The same is true of spiritual warfare. In the battle for the minds and souls of men, the enemy is Satan—and the untold number of demons who are at his command. If we are in Jesus, our ultimate victory over evil is assured. Still, Satan has the power to disarm us, oppress us, even kill us if we choose to remain naive about his activity on earth and in the lives of men.

Just who is Satan? What are demons?

Most people today—even most Christians—have trouble believing in an unseen spiritual enemy. That's Satan's most powerful tactic—convincing Christians that he and his demons do not exist. If he can do that, then the demons can continue their evil work without interference or opposition from the very ones who have authority over them—believers.

Jesus believed in demons. He assumed that His audiences believed in them. Not only did He teach about them, but He spent a significant part of His ministry casting demons out of people who were possessed by them. He recognized their power to harass, possess, and destroy. Yet He always exhibited complete authority over them—an authority which is also ours through Him.

Before we can look at how Jesus battled the demons and how we, like Him, can overcome them in spiritual warfare, we need to see what the Bible has to say about our enemy.

2. THE ORIGIN OF SATAN

Bible scholars point to two Old Testament passages, Isaiah 14:11-17 and Ezekiel 28:11-19, as key to understanding the origin of Satan and his demons.

READ THESE TWO PASSAGES, THEN MARK THE STATEMENTS FROM THE FOLLOWING LIST THAT ARE TRUE:

_____ Satan was an angelic being of great stature in heaven.

_____ He had a special anointing from God.

_____ He was evil from the start.

_____ His heart became full of pride.

_____ He wanted to be like God.

_____ God allowed him to remain in heaven.

_____ He was cast out of heaven to the earth.

The story continues in the book of Revelation. While the language is highly symbolic, most scholars agree that the picture being described here is that of the war in heaven in which Satan rebelled against God and was defeated.

WHO WAS HURLED TO THE EARTH WITH SATAN? (Rev. 12:9).

_____

HOW MANY ANGELS (REFERRED TO AS "STARS") WERE FLUNG TO EARTH WITH HIM? (Rev. 12:4).

_____ all of them

_____ 1/3 of them

_____ 144,000

In summary, then, we know that Satan was originally known as Lucifer, a mighty and beautiful archangel—the highest of God's created beings—anointed by God to lead the musical worship in heaven. However, Lucifer became prideful and wanted to be like God—to take God's place on the throne of heaven. He led an unsuccessful rebellion. God's retribution was swift. Now known as Satan, Lucifer was banished from heaven and forced—along with the one-third of the angelic host who followed him—to wander the earth until Jesus returns and casts him into hell.

HOW IS SATAN REFERRED TO IN THE FOLLOWING PASSAGES?

JOHN 16:11 _____

II COR. 4:4 _____

EPH. 2:2 _____

While Satan does not own the earth—it belongs to God—the scriptures clearly indicate that Satan has made himself head of the "cosmos" or present world system. He is the real, though invisible, power behind the world rulers. He was the power behind Tyre, behind Babylon, behind Greece and behind Rome. Undoubtedly, he is also the power behind many of our contemporary nations.

Other passages of scripture tell us more about our enemy—what he's like, his character.

WHAT DO THESE PASSAGES TELL US ABOUT SATAN?

John 8:44 _____

John 10:10 _____

II Cor. 11:14 _____

I Pet. 5:8 _____

THE WORD "SATAN" ACTUALLY MEANS "ACCUSER." WHAT DOES REVELATION 12:10 TELL US ABOUT SATAN'S ACTIVITIES?

_____

Satan is a liar and a murderer. He wants to kill us, to deceive us. He whispers lies to us. He heaps false guilt upon us. He causes us to waste time and money and to make bad decisions—thereby stealing from us and making us poor. He makes us sick. He wants to destroy our witness and make us ineffective Christians. He puts us into bondage.

3. DEMONS

Demons—the angels who fell with Satan—are tormented, tragic, pathetic creatures who follow a cruel master. They have no purpose, no place to call home. They wander the earth, seeking habitation. The Bible indicates that they can possess men and women—and even inhabit other living things.

EVEN AFTER A DEMON IS CAST OUT OF A PERSON, HE MAY SEEK TO RETURN. WHY? (Luke 11:24-26).

_____

WHO DID THE DEMON BRING WITH HIM WHEN HE RETURNED? (Luke 11:24-26).

_____

_____

WHEN JESUS COMMANDED THE DEMONS TO LEAVE THE GADARENE MADMAN, WHERE DID THEY BEG HIM TO LET THEM GO? (Mark 5:12).

_____

The Bible indicates that demons are organized into a hierarchy—not unlike a military command.

WHOM DOES THE APOSTLE PAUL SAY OUR BATTLE IS WITH? (Eph. 6:12).

_____

_____

_____

According to Paul, the enemy is organized into a hierarchy of "rulers," "authorities," and "powers." Demons may actually be assigned control over individuals, over cities, over entire nations or geographic regions. That latter concept is illustrated in Daniel 10:12-14.

WHAT CAUSED THE ANGEL TO BE DELAYED IN COMING TO ANSWER DANIEL'S PRAYER? (Dan. 10:13).

_____

The "prince of the Persian kingdom" was a demon assigned control over the entire geographic region of ancient Persia. Undoubtedly, he is still there—for that area is now the warring nations of Iran and Iraq.

4. WHAT DEMONS CAN DO TO CHRISTIANS

The Gospels are full of accounts of individuals who were possessed by demons—that is, the demons had taken total control over the person's mind, body, and spirit. While Christians cannot be totally possessed by a demon—as long as Jesus is on the throne of the believer's heart, no demon can reside there—demons can still cause Christians great torment. As Bible teacher Don Basham used to say, a Christian can have anything he wants to—including a demon. That is why the scriptures warn us to be alert, to avoid sin, and to shun even the appearance of evil. If we invite a demon in—he'll come in.

WHAT WARNINGS DO WE FIND IN THE FOLLOWING SCRIPTURES?

II Corinthians 2:10-11 _____

_____

Ephesians 4:26-27 _____

_____

WHAT PROMISES FOR CHRISTIANS ARE FOUND IN THE FOLLOWING PASSAGES?

John 6:37, 40 _____

_____

_____

_____

Romans 8:37-39 _____

_____

_____

_____

II Thessalonians 3:3 _____

_____

If demons cannot possess Christians, what can they do? They can move into our minds and *tempt* us—deceiving us into making horrible decisions. They can *dominate* us, driving us into compulsive behaviors—alcoholism, gluttony, nail-biting—anything over which we have lost control. And they can *afflict* us, causing sickness and—if we give in to the sickness and do not take authority over it—cause us to die.

5. OUR VICTORY

Jesus always displayed complete authority over demons. With a simple command from the Son of God, a demon—even the legion of demons who possessed the Gadarene man—was forced to flee from the person in whom it resided. We have that same authority today.

WHAT AUTHORITY DID JESUS GIVE TO HIS DISCIPLES?   (Matthew 10:1).

_____

AFTER HIS DEATH AND RESURRECTION, WHAT DID JESUS SAY WAS THE FIRST SIGN THAT WOULD ACCOMPANY THOSE OF US WHO BELIEVE IN HIM? (Mark 16:17)

_____

WHERE IS THE BELIEVER'S STRENGTH? (Ephesians 6:10).

_____

HOW DO WE PREPARE TO DEFEAT SATAN? (Ephesians 6:11).

_____

WHAT PROMISE OF VICTORY DO WE FIND IN I JOHN 4:4?

_____

_____

In Hebrews 2:14-15?

_____

_____

_____

What is God's final plan for Satan and his demons? (Matthew 25:41)

_____

_____

6. WRAP UP

Satan and his demons are real, and they are on a collision course with every believer in Christ. We cannot avoid the battle. We are already engaged in it.

What is our defense? Simply this: The authority of Jesus Christ—and the full armor of God. In future lessons, we'll learn how to put on that armor and use it to defeat the enemy.

7. FINAL LESSON

Satan and his demons are a formidable—but ultimately defeated—enemy. Jesus has provided His followers with all they need to be victorious in spiritual warfare.

8. PERSONAL REVIEW QUESTIONS

Circle T (true) or F (false)

1. T F Satan was once a mighty and beautiful angel.

2. T F Satan was cast out of heaven because God was jealous of him.

3. T F Satan does not own the earth, but he does have control over our world systems.

4. T F Satan often disguises himself as an angel of light.

5. T F Jesus did not believe in demons.

6. T F All a Christian needs to do is ignore a demon and it will go away.

7. T F Some demons have control over entire geographic regions.

8. T F Our battle is against flesh and blood.

9. T F Christians have the authority to cast out demons in Jesus' name.

10. T F Christians need to fear Satan because he has more power at his disposal than they do.

9. MEMORY VERSE

Ephesians 6:10-11 (Memorize, then write it on these lines.)

_____

_____

_____

_____

_____

10. PRACTICAL EXERCISE

THIS WEEK LIST THREE WAYS SATAN AND HIS DEMONS ATTACK YOU.

1. _____

_____

_____

2. _____

_____

_____

3. _____

_____

_____

TRUE OR FALSE ANSWERS:

1-T, 2-F, 3-T, 4-T, 5-F, 6-F, 7-T, 8-T, 9-T, 10-F

NOTES

LESSON 3
ANGELS
VIDEO REFERENCE: #3

1. INTRODUCTION

In warfare, we have said, it is important to know who your enemy is. It is just as important, however, to know who your allies are—whom you can depend on to stand and fight with you when the going gets tough.

In our last lesson we studied about Satan and his demons—the dark enemy forces in the unseen spiritual battle in which we are engaged. But countering those demons—in fact, far outnumbering them—are mighty forces of light, our allies in spiritual warfare—the angels.

Angels are the highest of God's created beings. They are immortal spirits, designed to serve and minister to their Creator. But in addition to ministering directly to God in heaven, they also have many purposes or assignments that impact the lives of men and women on earth.

2. MESSENGER ANGELS

The term angel—"angelos" in Greek—means, simply, "messenger." The Bible records numerous examples of angels being sent by God to present a particular message to someone on earth.

Perhaps the best known examples are found in the stories surrounding the births of John the Baptist and of Jesus.

WHO APPEARED TO ZECHARIAH TO TELL HIM HE WOULD BECOME A FATHER IN HIS OLD AGE? (Luke 1:11, 19)

_____

WHO CAME TO MARY TO TELL HER SHE WOULD BEAR A SON BY THE HOLY SPIRIT? (Luke 1:26-28)

_____

The angel who appeared to Zechariah and to Mary was named Gabriel, the archangel over all the messenger angels.

WHERE DOES GABRIEL STAND WHEN HE IS NOT DELIVERING MESSAGES? (Luke 1:19)

_____

WHO SENDS HIM TO DELIVER HIS MESSAGES? (Luke 1:19; 1:26)

_____

WHO TOLD THE SHEPHERDS ABOUT THE BIRTH OF JESUS? (Luke 2:8-12)

_____

HOW WAS THIS VISITATION DIFFERENT FROM THE ONES TO MARY AND ZECHARIAH? (Luke 2:13-14)

_____

_____

WHAT WAS THE COMMON REACTION OF ZECHARIAH, MARY AND THE SHEPHERDS UPON SEEING THE ANGELS? (Luke 1:12; 1:29; 2:9)

_____ They jumped for joy and praised the Lord.

_____ They were amazed and frightened.

_____ They told the angels to go away and leave them alone.

Apparently, it can be a frightening thing to come face to face with an angel in all its glory.

WHAT WAS THE COMMON RESPONSE OF THE ANGELS? (Luke 1:13; 1:30; 2:10)

_____ They felt unwanted and left.

_____ They told them not to be afraid, that God had sent them.

_____ They ridiculed the people for being frightened.

Not all angels appear to men in such awesome form, however.

WHAT WARNING DOES PAUL GIVE IN HEBREWS 13:2?

_____

_____

3. MINISTERING ANGELS

Sometimes angels are sent by God to minister to us when we are in deep need.

WHO DOES THE WRITER OF HEBREWS SAY THAT ANGELS ARE? (Hebrews 1:14)

_____

WHOM ARE THEY SENT TO SERVE? (Hebrews 1:14)

_____

Two Bible passages in particular record Jesus in times of great distress.

WHAT DO THESE ACCOUNTS HAVE IN COMMON? (Matthew 4:11; Luke 22:43)

_____

_____

The Old Testament also records the activity of ministering angels. I Kings 19 tells the story of the prophet Elijah fleeing from the wicked Queen Jezebel. In deep despair, Elijah collapsed under a tree at the edge of the desert and begged God to take his life.

HOW DID THE ANGEL MINISTER TO ELIJAH? (I Kings 19:5-9)

_____

_____

4. GUARDIAN ANGELS

Angels may also be assigned to protect us from harm and to rescue us from danger.

When Satan tried to tempt Jesus to throw Himself from the pinnacle of the temple, he quoted Psalm 91:11-12.

WHAT PROMISE IS FOUND IN THAT PASSAGE? (See also Luke 4:10-11)

_____

_____

_____

WHAT PROMISE IS FOUND IN PSALM 34:7?

_____

_____

WHO TOLD JOSEPH TO ESCAPE TO EGYPT WITH THE BABY JESUS, AND WHY? (Matthew 2:13)

_____

_____

_____

HOW WAS THE APOSTLE PETER RESCUED FROM PRISON? (Acts 12:5-11)

_____

_____

WHY DID JESUS TELL HIS DISCIPLES NOT TO UNDERESTIMATE THE IMPORTANCE OF CHILDREN TO THE FATHER? (Matthew 18:10)

_____

_____

HOW WONDERFUL IT IS TO KNOW THAT EVERY CHILD HAS A GUARDIAN ANGEL WATCHING OVER HIM!

5. WARRING ANGELS

Of all the angels, none are more important than the warring angels—those angels who fight off the evil spirits, who actually enter into combat in the invisible realm called "the heavenlies" to protect us from the onslaughts of Satan and his army of demons.

WHEN SATAN LED HIS REBELLION IN HEAVEN, WHO LED GOD'S OPPOSITION FORCES? (Revelation 12:7)

_____

WHO WON THE BATTLE? (Revelation 12:7-9)

_____

_____

In our last lesson we looked at Daniel 10, in which a messenger angel carrying an answer to Daniel's prayer was blocked by a demon called the "prince of Persia."

WHO DID THE ANGEL CALL ON FOR HELP IN BATTLING THE PERSIAN DEMON? (Daniel 10:13)

_____

WHO WON THAT SKIRMISH? (Daniel 10:13-14)

_____

Michael is the archangel of the warring angels—the commanding officer in God's angelic army. It is a mighty army, poised and ready to fight on behalf of God's elect—His believers on earth. Because of our limited faculties, we are usually not aware of this tremendous fighting force surrounding us. However, in at least one instance recorded in the Old Testament, a man's spiritual eyes were opened to see the angels prepared to battle on his behalf.

Two men—the prophet Elisha and his servant—were pitted against an army of Syrian warriors.

YET WHO DID ELISHA SAY HAD THE NUMERICAL ADVANTAGE? (II Kings 6:16)

_____

WHAT DID THE SERVANT SEE AFTER ELISHA PRAYED THAT HIS EYES BE OPENED? (II Kings 6:17)

_____

_____

When Jesus was about to be arrested by the Roman soldiers, Peter drew his sword to fight. But Jesus told him to put down his weapon.

WHO DID JESUS SAY WOULD HAVE BEEN IMMEDIATELY DISPATCHED TO FIGHT FOR HIM IF HE HAD BUT SAID THE WORD? (Matthew 26:53)

_____

_____

We learned in our last lesson that one-third of the angels in heaven rebelled with Satan and were cast to the earth with him (Revelation 12:4)—becoming the demons and evil spirits we battle today. That means that two-thirds of the angels remained loyal to God and fight with us in spiritual warfare. That's twice as many angels as demons!

6. OUR RELATIONSHIP TO THE ANGELS

WHEN THE SON OF GOD HUMBLED HIMSELF AND BECAME A MAN, DID THAT MAKE HIM HIGHER OR LOWER THAN THE ANGELS IN GOD'S CREATIVE ORDER? (Hebrews 2:9)

_____ higher

_____ lower

AFTER JESUS' RESURRECTION, HOW DID THAT ORDER CHANGE? (I Peter 3:22)

_____

_____

IF WE ARE IN CHRIST, WHERE ARE WE SEATED? (Ephesians 2:6)

_____

WHAT DOES I CORINTHIANS 6:3 INFER ABOUT THE BELIEVER'S FINAL POSITION IN RELATION TO THE ANGELS?

_____

_____

WHAT WARNING CONCERNING OUR RELATIONSHIP TO ANGELS IS INCLUDED IN COLOSSIANS 2:18?

_____

7. WRAP UP

As Christians, we rarely see the host of angels who minister to us, guard us, fight for us—and that is probably for the best, since we are to look to God, not to angels, for our hope and strength. Still, God intends for us to be comforted and encouraged in the knowledge that we are not alone in the battle against the evil forces on earth. Our allies are the angels—a mighty army prepared and equipped to fight with us and for us in spiritual warfare.

8. FINAL LESSON

God has given us every resource necessary to be victorious in the spiritual battles we face—including access to the angels in heaven. Our task is to pray—and leave the battle to God.

9. PERSONAL REVIEW QUESTIONS

Circle T (true) or F (false)

1. T   F   Man has never actually seen an angel.

2. T   F   Angels have played an important role in God's plan throughout history.

3. T   F   You would definitely know it if you saw an angel.

4. T   F   The angels ministered to Jesus at several points during His life on earth.

5. T   F   Since angels are higher than men in God's creative order, it is presumptive to expect that angels would minister to us.

6.   T   F   Angels have been known to rescue believers from danger or harm.

7.   T   F   Jesus did not ask God to send the angels to help Him because He knew God would deny the request.

8.   T   F   In the war that took place in heaven, the archangel Michael and his army defeated Satan and his rebellious forces.

9.   T   F   There are more angels fighting for us than there are demons fighting against us.

10.   T   F   We should worship angels because they are so much higher and greater than we are.

10. MEMORY VERSE

Ephesians 6:10-12 (Memorize, then write it on these lines.)

_____

_____

_____

_____

_____

11. PRACTICAL EXERCISE

This week:

1. RECALL ANY EXPERIENCE (PAST OR PRESENT) WHEN YOU'VE SEEN, HEARD, OR BEEN AWARE OF AN ANGEL PRESENCE:

_____

_____

_____

_____

_____

2. TELL OF ONE EXPERIENCE DURING THIS WEEK WHEN YOU CALLED ON ANGELS TO HELP YOU:

_____

_____

_____

_____

_____

TRUE OR FALSE ANSWERS:

1-F, 2-T, 3-F, 4-T, 5-F, 6-T, 7-F, 8-T, 9-T, 10-F

LESSON 4
THE BELT OF TRUTH
VIDEO REFERENCE: #4

1. INTRODUCTION

Warfare is serious business. A good soldier knows that—and never goes into battle unprepared. Proper preparation, with the necessary equipment for combat, can mean the difference between victory and defeat—even between life and death.

The same is true for spiritual warfare. It's serious business. Yet Christians tend to underestimate—or overlook completely—the spiritual armor God has provided. We choose to go into battle unprepared. No wonder so many of us get battered and bloodied when Satan attacks!

In our first lesson, we looked briefly at the apostle Paul's instructions on "dressing for success" in spiritual warfare. Now we will begin to look at the spiritual armor available to us more closely, piece by piece.

2. TAKING OUR STAND

Paul describes this armor in Ephesians 6:10-18.

WHERE DO WE FIND OUR STRENGTH FOR THE BATTLE? (Ephesians 6:10)

_____

IS THE FOLLOWING STATEMENT TRUE OR FALSE? (Ephesians 6:11)

Since God is our power and strength, Christians have no active role in spiritual warfare.

_____ True

_____ False

WHAT DOES PAUL TELL US TO DO? (Ephesians 6:11 & 13)

_____

WHY SHOULD WE DO THIS? (Ephesians 6:11 & 13)

_____

_____

SHOULD WE PUT ON OUR ARMOR BEFORE OR AFTER WE FIND OURSELVES UNDER ATTACK? (Ephesians 6:13)

_____ before

_____ after

The word "stand" appears _____ number of times in verses 11-14.

WHEN WE ARE UNDER ATTACK, WHICH OF THE FOLLOWING SHOULD WE DO?

_____ turn and retreat until we secure a safe position

_____ take the offensive and counterattack

_____ dig our feet in and hold our ground

Stand means simply this: stand. It does not mean flee. It does not mean fight back. It means we are to hold our ground when we are under attack. Stand means that every morning when we wake up, we dress ourselves in God's armor. Then we let the angels fight the battle in the heavenlies. If we have our armor on, it doesn't matter how, when, or where Satan attacks; we're prepared. We can take it.

Other Bible writers also encourage Christians to stand.

WHAT WORD IS USED INSTEAD OF "STAND," BUT WITH SIMILAR MEANING, IN THE FOLLOWING PASSAGES?

I Peter 5:8-9 _____

James 4:7 _____

WHAT MUST THE DEVIL DO WHEN WE RESIST HIM? (James 4:7)

3. THE BELT OF TRUTH

WHAT IS THE FIRST PIECE OF ARMOR WE SHOULD PUT ON? (Ephesians 6:14)

_____

In Jesus' day, the foundational piece of armor worn by a Roman soldier was the belt, or girdle—a wide garment worn across the lower torso. It served two purposes: it held the sword, and it protected the "loins" (that portion of the body extending from mid-thigh to the ribcage).

In ancient Israel, men did not wear trousers; they wore long, loose robes, which provided a natural "air conditioning" in the desert heat. However, this was poor battle garb. So as the first step in preparing to go to war, a man "girded his loins"—which essentially means he "tucked his cloak into his belt." With his loins girded, he had greater mobility and quickness. He was ready for the fight.

For the Christian soldier, truth is that foundational armor. When we put on the belt of truth, we are serving notice that we are ready. We're committing ourselves to the battle. We're taking the first step toward warfare, and we're not turning back.

4. WHAT IS TRUTH?

WHAT QUESTION DID PILATE, THE ROMAN GOVERNOR, ASK OF JESUS BEFORE TURNING HIM OVER TO BE CRUCIFIED? (John 18:38)

_____

Pilate's question is still valid today. If we're going to put on the belt of truth, we must know what truth is—and what it is not.

In Greek, the language of the New Testament, the word "truth" has two related meanings. The first is, basically, the lack of falsehood—the essence or reality of a matter. A thing is either true or it's a lie. As Christians, we need to know what is true regarding God, His Son, and the major tenets of our faith. If we know what the scriptures say about a matter, then Satan cannot tempt us or mislead us with a lie.

WHAT DID JESUS SAY TRUTH IS? (John 17:17)

_____

_____

The downfall of mankind was precipitated when the first woman, Eve, doubted God's word and believed Satan's lie.

HOW DOES JOHN 8:44 DESCRIBE SATAN?

_____

_____

_____

WHAT DID GOD SAY WOULD HAPPEN TO ADAM AND EVE IF THEY ATE FROM THE TREE OF THE KNOWLEDGE OF GOOD AND EVIL? (Genesis 2:17)

_____

_____

WHAT LIE DID SATAN TELL EVE? (Genesis 3:1, 4)

_____

_____

The Greek word translated "schemes" or "wiles" of the devil in Ephesians 6:11 is translated "cunning and craftiness" in Ephesians 4:14. It is referring to doctrines or teachings that are cunningly misrepresented.

WHAT DO THE FOLLOWING PASSAGES SAY ABOUT THE DANGER OF BEING UNCERTAIN ABOUT OUR BELIEFS?

Matthew 7:15 _____

_____

_____

Ephesians 4:14 _____

_____

WHAT BASIC MISTAKE WAS MADE BY THE PEOPLE IN THE FOLLOWING PASSAGES?

Romans 1:18-25 _____

_____

II Timothy 4:3-4 _____

_____

WHAT DID JESUS SAY WILL HAPPEN IF WE HOLD TO HIS TEACHINGS?
(John 8:31-32)

_____

_____

WHO WILL HELP US TO KNOW WHAT IS TRUE AND WHAT IS NOT? (John
16:13)

_____

It is not enough to simply know the truth. Scripture encourages us to do
something with it.

WHAT DO THE FOLLOWING PASSAGES TELL US WE SHOULD DO WITH
TRUTH?

I Corinthians 13:6 _____

Philippians 4:8 _____

II Thessalonians 2:10 _____

II Timothy 2:15 _____

I Peter 1:22 _____

III John 3 _____

If we are going to stand against the attacks of Satan, we must know the
truth—and we must hold on to it. Otherwise, we are ineffective soldiers,
constantly being taken advantage of by those who would lead us away
from the pure gospel of Jesus Christ. Error in the church divides the body
of Christ and weakens the spiritual warriors. When we believe Satan's lies,
we put chinks in our armor—and we are no longer protected from demons.

5. TRUTH IN THE INNER PARTS

The second meaning for the Greek word "truth" is broader than simply the lack of falsehood; it refers to "truthfulness," a sincerity and integrity of character.

WHAT DOES PSALM 51:6 SAY GOD DESIRES?

_____

_____

_____

In this psalm, in which David was asking forgiveness for his sexual sin, "inner parts" refers specifically to the loins. The loins—where sexual sin takes place—get God's people in more trouble than any other part of the body—unless it's the tongue. Girding the loins, in this very real sense, then, is a critical part of the Christian's armor.

However, having "truth in the inner parts" can also refer to having truth at a deeper level—being truthful in character, down to the deepest parts of our being.

HOW DID THE APOSTLE JOHN DESCRIBE JESUS' CHARACTER? (John 1:14)

_____

WHAT DID JESUS SAY ABOUT HIMSELF IN JOHN 14:6?

_____

_____

What does it mean to be a "truthful" person—to be truth, as Jesus was? It means we do not lie to ourselves, to others, or to God. We do not lie in word—or in deed. The Bible teaches that when we become Christians, we "put on" Christ. Truth, then, is wearing the character and the nature of Jesus around the middle of our bodies. If we put on Jesus, then He will show us exactly what to do. We will become a God-person in our neighborhood, our prison wing, our business, our classroom.

By this definition, truth and facts are not always the same thing. A story in Matthew 18:23-35 illustrates the difference.

HOW MUCH DID THE SERVANT OWE THE KING? (Matthew 18:24)

_____

WHAT WAS THE SERVANT'S RIGHTFUL PUNISHMENT? (Matthew 18:25)

_____

WHAT DID THE KING DO INSTEAD? (Matthew 18:27)

_____

HOW MUCH DID THE SECOND SERVANT OWE THE FIRST SERVANT? (Matthew 18:28)

_____

WHAT DID THE FIRST SERVANT DO TO THE ONE WHO OWED HIM MONEY? (Matthew 18:30)

_____

_____

WHY WAS THE KING UPSET ABOUT WHAT THE FIRST SERVANT HAD DONE? (Matthew 18:32-33)

_____

_____

The facts were these: The second servant *did* owe the first one money. The lender did have the right to call in his debt. He also had the right under the law to have the debtor thrown into jail when he couldn't pay up. But the truth was this: The first servant had been forgiven a great debt. Therefore, he had an obligation to forgive also.

6. WRAP UP

The belt of truth is the first piece of armor God tells us to take up if we are going to stand against the devil's schemes. That means, before we do anything else, we need to be sure we are believing—and holding fast to—the truth that is revealed in God's Word. Then, with God's help, we need to act as people of integrity, walking out daily a life that is consistent with the nature and character of Jesus. If we do that, Satan will not be able to tempt us with deception or persuade us with lies.

7. FINAL LESSON

Truth is not simply something you believe; it is something you live.

8. PERSONAL REVIEW QUESTIONS

Circle T (true) or F (false)

1. T F There's no way to prepare for an attack from Satan.
2. T F We should put on the belt of truth as soon as Satan attacks.
3. T F When Satan attacks, we should stand our ground.
4. T F When we resist the devil, he fights back even harder.
5. T F Adam and Eve sinned because they did not know what the truth was.
6. T F There are people who will take advantage of you if you are not sure of what you believe.
7. T F The Holy Spirit will lead us to truth.
8. T F We are to love, obey, and rejoice in the truth.
9. T F Jesus was the perfect example of a "truthful" person.
10. T F The best way to be a truthful person is to stick to the facts.

9. MEMORY VERSE

Ephesians 6:10-13 (Memorize, then write it on these lines.)

_____

_____

_____

_____

_____

_____

_____

10. PRACTICAL EXERCISE

THIS WEEK NOTE AN EXPERIENCE IN WHICH YOU ARE TEMPTED TO DISTORT THE TRUTH—BUT DO NOT:

_____

_____

_____

_____

_____

TRUE OR FALSE ANSWERS:

1-F, 2-F, 3-T, 4-F, 5-F, 6-T, 7-T, 8-T, 9-T, 10-F

NOTES

NOTES

LESSON 5
THE BREASTPLATE OF RIGHTEOUSNESS
VIDEO REFERENCE: #5

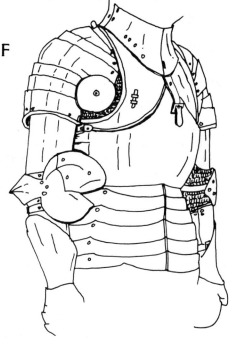

1. INTRODUCTION

As we continue to study the spiritual armor God has provided to assure victory in the war against Satan, we now move to the "breastplate of righteousness." After we have buckled on the belt of truth—grounding ourselves in God's word and putting on the character of Jesus—we must pick up the breastplate of righteousness and secure it tightly, for it is a critical factor in our defense.

2. THE BREASTPLATE OF RIGHTEOUSNESS

WHAT IS THE SECOND PIECE OF ARMOR PAUL TELLS US TO PUT ON? (Ephesians 6:14)

_____

A Roman soldier wore a large breastplate to provide front-to-back coverage for his heart and bowels—those vital organs which, if struck by an enemy sword, could be fatally wounded. To the Jew of that day, the heart represented the mind—what we think. The bowels represented the emotions—what we feel. And just as our heart and digestive organs are critical to the bodily functions required for life, so our thoughts and our feelings are critical to who we are—and how effective we are—in Jesus Christ.

They are also the key areas where Satan attacks us, since he knows that to control our thoughts and feelings is to control us. He wants to drive a sword into our minds, filling them with lies, perversion, immorality and untruth. He wants to confuse our emotions, making us fearful, filled with doubt and lustful after the wrong things. But God has provided us with perfect protection. He's given us the breastplate of righteousness.

3. FILTHY RAGS

A basic definition for righteousness is "the character or quality of being right or just." It is the quality which puts us in a right standing with God. A righteous man is one who does everything God requires him to do—who is everything God requires him to be.

The Pharisees of Jesus' day were those religious people who worked very hard at being righteous. They observed every feast and ceremony and obeyed every one of God's laws to the letter—they even made up new laws, since, when it came to righteousness, they didn't wanted to leave anything to guesswork.

JESUS SAID THAT IF WE WANT TO ENTER THE KINGDOM OF HEAVEN, OUR RIGHTEOUSNESS MUST (Matthew 5:20):

_____ come close to that of the Pharisees

_____ equal that of the Pharisees

_____ exceed that of the Pharisees

The Pharisees did everything they could do—and more—to be righteous. But apparently it wasn't enough. There is a difference between being right and being righteous. The Pharisees were right—it was right to obey the laws of God—but they were not righteous.

WHY DID JESUS COMPARE THE PHARISEES TO WHITEWASHED TOMBS? (Matthew 23:27-28)

_____

_____

Before his conversion to Christ, the Apostle Paul was a Pharisee, confident of his right standing with God.

LIST FIVE REASONS PAUL GAVE FOR HIS CONFIDENCE IN THE FLESH: (Philippians 3:4-6)

1. _____

2. _____

3. _____

4. _____

5. _____

After becoming a Christian, Paul realized that his confidence had been misplaced.

WHAT DID PAUL CALL THOSE THINGS IN WHICH HE HAD FORMERLY PLACED HIS CONFIDENCE? (Philippians 3:8)

_____

HOW DOES GOD VIEW OUR ATTEMPTS TO BE RIGHTEOUS? (Isaiah 64:6)

_____

No matter how hard we try, there is no way to make ourselves righteous—to work ourselves into a right relationship with God. There is always something blocking the way—and that thing is sin.

HOW DOES SIN EFFECT OUR RELATIONSHIP WITH GOD? (Isaiah 59:2)

_____

_____

HOW MANY HAVE SINNED AND MISSED GOD'S MARK FOR THEM? (Romans 3:23)

_____ none of us

_____ most of us

_____ all of us

ACCORDING TO ROMANS 3:10, WHO IS RIGHTEOUS?

_____ none of us

_____ most of us

_____ all of us

4. THE RIGHTEOUSNESS THAT COMES FROM GOD

Paul said that he did not want a righteousness of his own that came from following the law. He knew that all his efforts to be righteous were merely "rubbish" and "filthy rags" in God's sight.

WHAT KIND OF RIGHTEOUSNESS DID PAUL WANT? (Philippians 3:9)

_____

HOW DO WE GET THIS KIND OF RIGHTEOUSNESS? (Philippians 3:9)

_____

WHO GIVES IT TO US? (Philippians 3:9)

_____

Romans 3:21-26 expands on this same theme.

UPON WHOM DOES GOD CONFER RIGHTEOUSNESS? (Romans 3:22)

_____

TO BE MADE RIGHTEOUS BY GOD, IN WHOM MUST WE PLACE OUR FAITH? (Romans 3:22)

_____

When the Son of God hung on the cross and died, His shed blood fulfilled God's requirement that a sacrifice be made for the remission of sin. As the Perfect Sacrifice, His death paid the price once and for all for the sins of the world—including yours and mine.

WHAT DID JESUS DO FOR US? (Romans 5:8)

_____

_____

WHAT DID JESUS BECOME FOR US? (II Corinthians 5:21)

_____

_____

WHY? (II Corinthians 5:21)

_____

_____

WHAT HAS JUSTIFIED US IN GOD'S SIGHT? (Romans 5:9)

_____

_____

WHAT PURIFIES US FROM SIN? (I John 1:7)

_____

WHAT DOES ROMANS 5:18-19 SAY GOD HAS DONE THROUGH THE SACRIFICE OF JESUS?

_____

_____

WHAT IS OUR RELATIONSHIP TO GOD WHEN WE BELIEVE IN JESUS? (John 1:12-13)

_____ we are His slaves

_____ we are His friends

_____ we are His children

What does righteousness mean? Simply this: not guilty. Jesus paid the price for our sin by the shedding of His blood. We are "not guilty" no matter what the accuser, Satan, whispers to the contrary. Righteousness means we now have a right relationship with God—not because of anything we are or anything we've done, but because of Who Jesus is and what He's done. Through faith in Him, His righteousness becomes ours, and we become sons and daughters of God.

5. RIGHTEOUSNESS IN PRACTICE

Since our righteousness is found in Jesus and not in the things we do for God, do we need to be concerned with living a right and just life? The scriptures answer a resounding: Yes!

ROMANS 6:15-16 SAYS WE ARE EITHER SLAVES TO SIN, WHICH LEADS

TO_____

OR SLAVES TO OBEDIENCE TO GOD, WHICH LEADS TO

_____

SINCE WE HAVE BEEN SET FREE FROM THE CONTROL OF SIN THROUGH THE SHED BLOOD OF JESUS, TO WHAT SHOULD WE COMMIT OUR LIVES? (Romans 6:19)

_____

WHEN WE BECOME CHRISTIANS, WHAT DO WE "PUT OFF"? (Ephesians 4:22)

_____

_____

WHAT DO WE "PUT ON"? (Ephesians 4:24)

_____

_____

WHAT IS THE NEW SELF CREATED TO BE LIKE? (Ephesians 4:24)

_____

_____

In the passage we have just looked at in Ephesians, we are encouraged to live out the new, righteous nature God has given us in Christ. How do we do this? Paul tells us beginning in verse 25: "Therefore. . . .." We are new, righteous creatures; *therefore* we have things to do. He goes on to tell what some of those things are in the remainder of Ephesians.

LIST 8 OF THE THINGS PAUL TELLS US TO DO IN EPHESIANS 4:25-5:21.

1. _____

2. _____

3. _____

4. _____

5. _____

6. _____

   _____

7. _____

   _____

8. _____

If we live righteously, our thoughts and feelings will be protected from Satan's attack.

WHAT DO THE FOLLOWING SCRIPTURES ENCOURAGE US TO DO?

Colossians 3:1-2 _____

_____

_____

Philippians 4:6 _____

_____

_____

Philippians 4:8 _____

_____

_____

_____

6. WRAP UP

Remember, we're talking about spiritual warfare, and about putting on the breastplate of righteousness—that piece of armor designed to protect our minds and emotions from demonic attack. We do that first by reminding ourselves daily—and testifying to Satan—that the penalty for our sin has been paid for by the blood of Jesus. We're not guilty! We have a right standing with God because of what Jesus did for us at Calvary. Nothing Satan can do will rob us of that.

We also put on the breastplate by seeking to live righteously—like sons and daughters of God. If our thoughts are turned to Jesus and our feelings are overflowing with the desire to please our Heavenly Father, then no dart or arrow from the enemy will ever be able to hit its mark.

7. FINAL LESSON

Because Jesus Christ has become our righteousness, we can live right and just lives and defeat the enemy.

8. PERSONAL REVIEW QUESTIONS

Circle T (true) or F (false)

1. T   F   The breastplate of righteousness is capable of protecting our thoughts and feelings from being controlled by Satan.

2. T   F   We are made righteous by the good things we do.

3. T   F   Paul was righteous because he was born into a good Hebrew family and obeyed all of God's laws.

4. T   F   Jesus called the Pharisees hypocrites because they were righteous in their outward actions but not in their inward beings.

5. T   F   The Bible sayings, "None are righteous" and "All have sinned," are not referring to us.

6. T   F   When Jesus died on the cross He paid the penalty for our sin.

7. T   F   We are justified before God and purified from sin by the blood of Jesus.

8. T   F   It would be blasphemous for a Christian to call himself a son of God.

9. T   F   When we become Christians we become new men and women, created to live righteous lives.

10. T   F   We need to set our minds on the things of this world.

9. MEMORY VERSE

Ephesians 6:10-14 (Memorize, then write it on these lines.)

_____

_____

_____

_____

_____

_____

_____

10. PRACTICAL EXERCISE

Many people have a poor self image. Find one person who has a poor self image, who thinks God does not love him, and share the good news of II Corinthians 5:17.

Note how the person responds:

_____

_____

_____

TRUE OR FALSE ANSWERS:

1-T, 2-F, 3-F, 4-T, 5-F, 6-T, 7-T, 8-F, 9-T, 10-F

LESSON 6
THE SHOES OF READINESS
VIDEO REFERENCE: #6

I. INTRODUCTION

Shoes are a major part of our culture—a fashion item, available in a myriad of colors, styles and sizes to suit a multitude of purposes. But in Jesus' day, shoes served one major purpose: they protected the feet from the rough, sometimes dangerous, terrain of the Middle East. The soldier's shoe, in particular, had to take him long distances—over rocks and brambles, scorpions and snakes—and still keep him from slipping or stumbling when the battle got tough.

God tells Christians to wear a special kind of shoe, too, in the spiritual battle we're fighting. We can buckle on the belt of truth and put on the breastplate of righteousness, but if our feet aren't dressed correctly, we'll slip and fall.

2. THE GOSPEL OF PEACE

WHAT IS THE THIRD PIECE OF ARMOR PAUL TELLS US TO PUT ON? (Ephesians 6:15)

_____

_____

Paul tells us that the shoes of readiness come from "the gospel [good news] of peace." If we want to be sure we're putting the right shoes on, we need to know what "the good news of peace" is. We don't want to put on bedroom slippers if the occasion calls for hiking boots.

HOW DO THE FOLLOWING SCRIPTURES DESCRIBE THE RELATIONSHIP WE HAD WITH GOD BEFORE WE BELIEVED IN JESUS?

Romans 5:10 _____

_____

Colossians 1:21 _____

_____

ACCORDING TO THE FOLLOWING SCRIPTURES, HOW DID JESUS' DEATH
ON THE CROSS CHANGE THAT RELATIONSHIP?

Romans 5:10-11 _____

_____

Colossians 1:19-23 _____

_____

_____

_____

Since we have been justified by faith in Jesus, we now have _____

with God (Romans 5:1).

We are no longer enemies; we have peace with God! That's the good
news. God is on our side. Read Romans 8:31-39. Now that we are reconciled
to God, which of the following things has the power to separate us from
Him?

_____ death

_____ life

_____ angels

_____ demons and evil powers

_____ the present

_____ the future

_____ great heights

_____ great depths

If God is for us, who can be against us? For Paul, that's a rhetorical question.
He knew the answer: no one, not even Satan himself, can stand against
us if God is standing with us. When we fit our feet with the readiness
that comes from the gospel of peace, we remind ourselves—and testify
to Satan—that through Jesus our feet have been set firmly in God's camp.

3. BEAUTIFUL FEET

We need to put on the shoes of readiness so that we are prepared to
stand against the devil's schemes. But shoes are not just for standing. They're
for moving—for going places. When we fit our feet with the readiness
that comes from the gospel of peace, we're telling God, "My feet are ready
to go wherever you want me to go."

ACCORDING TO THE PROPHET ISAIAH, WHO HAS "BEAUTIFUL FEET"? (Isaiah 52:7 and Romans 10:15)

_____

_____

God doesn't want us to keep the good news of peace to ourselves. He wants us to be prepared to "announce peace" to our friends, our neighbors, our co-workers, the check-out person at the grocery store, and anyone else He causes to cross our path.

WHAT DO THE FOLLOWING SCRIPTURES ENCOURAGE US TO DO?

II Timothy 4:2 _____

_____

_____

I Peter 3:15 _____

_____

_____

One man who was always prepared to tell the good news of peace was Philip. Read Acts 8:26-40.

WHERE DID PHILIP GET HIS DIRECTIONS? (Acts 8:26 & 29)

_____

WHAT DID PHILIP TELL THE ETHIOPIAN EUNUCH? (Acts 8:35)

_____

WHAT HAPPENED TO PHILIP AFTER THE EUNUCH WAS BAPTIZED? (Acts 8:39)

_____

WHAT DID PHILIP DO WHEN HE APPEARED AT AZOTUS? (Acts 8:40)

_____

All of us may not be taken up by the Spirit and set down again elsewhere to preach the good news as Philip was. However, we all have to be ready to go where God wants us to go and say what God wants us to say. God was able to use Philip in the way that He did because Philip was prepared—his feet were always fitted with the readiness that comes from the gospel of peace.

4. GOING WHERE GOD WANTS US TO GO

The eleventh chapter of the book of Hebrews is the "Who's Who" of the Bible. The writer lists many of the great champions of faith who lived in Old Testament times. The first of those named is Abraham, the father of the Jewish race.

WHAT DID GOD CALL ABRAHAM TO DO? (Hebrews 11:8)

_____

_____

_____

HOW DID ABRAHAM RESPOND? (Hebrews 11:8)

_____

DID ABRAHAM KNOW WHERE HE WAS GOING BEFORE HE SET OUT? (Hebrews 11:8)

_____ Yes

_____ No

HOW DOES THE BIBLE SAY WE ARE TO LIVE? (II Corinthians 5:7)

_____

We need to trust God enough to take the first step He tells us to take—even if He hasn't revealed to us what our second and third steps will be. God will guide us, just as He has guided His people throughout history.

WHEN THE CHILDREN OF ISRAEL ESCAPED THE BONDAGE OF EGYPT AND MADE THEIR 40-YEAR TREK THROUGH THE WILDERNESS TO THE PROMISED LAND, HOW DID THEY KNOW WHAT DIRECTION TO TAKE? (Exodus 13:21)

_____

_____

_____

WHAT PROMISES REGARDING GOD'S GUIDANCE ARE CONTAINED IN THE FOLLOWING SCRIPTURES?

I Samuel 2:9 _____

_____

Psalm 56:13 _____

_____

_____

Luke 1:79 _____

_____

Most of the time we do not get our guidance from an angel or a pillar of fire. More often, God guides us in less dramatic, but equally certain, ways.

WHAT DOES THE PSALMIST CALL GOD'S WORD? (Psalm 119:105)

_____

_____

God gives direction through His Word, the Bible. He also speaks His word to us in the deep recesses of our hearts or consciences through His Spirit in us, often discernable as a gentle nudging or quiet suggestion.

HOW WILL WE KNOW WHICH WAY TO TURN? (Isaiah 30:21)

_____

_____

5. KEEPING IN STEP

In Galatians 5:25, Paul tells us we must keep in step with:

_____ the music

_____ other Christians

_____ the Spirit

Keeping in step with the Spirit is a way of life—a "walk." In Jesus' day, everyone walked. So when the Bible talks about our "walk," it's talking about our way of life. In fact, where some translations of the Bible read "walk," others read "life," and vice versa.

That means if we are daily seeking God's guidance for our lives through His Word, if we are regularly listening for the voice of His Spirit within us, there will be some things we will do—and some things we will not do. There will be some places we will go—and some places we will not go. Keeping in step with the Spirit changes our lifestyles.

NAME EIGHT OF THE FIFTEEN ACTIVITIES LISTED IN GALATIANS 5:19-21 WE WILL AVOID IF WE ARE LED BY THE SPIRIT.

1. _____

2. _____

3. _____

4. _____

5. _____

6. _____

7. _____

8. _____

WHAT QUALITIES WILL BEGIN TO SHOW UP IN OUR LIVES AS WE ARE LED BY THE SPIRIT? (Galatians 5:22-23)

1. _____

2. _____

3. _____

4. _____

5. _____

6. _____

7. _____

8. _____

9. _____

In Ephesians, Paul says that when we are led by the Spirit of God, we are "walking in the light."

WE SHOULD LIVE [WALK] AS CHILDREN OF_____
(Ephesians 5:8)

WE DO THAT BY IMITATING _____ (Ephesians 5:1)

HOW DOES JOHN DESCRIBE GOD IN I JOHN 1:5?

_____

_____

WHAT HAPPENS WHEN WE WALK IN THE LIGHT? (I John 1:7)

1. _____

2. _____

_____

Walking in the light means living a life that demonstrates the very nature of God, illuminated by the new perspective we have as His children.

WHAT IS JESUS' PROMISE IN JOHN 8:12?

_____

_____

When a room becomes full of light, the darkness is swept away. That's what happens when we walk in the light—Satan is forced to leave. There's no room for him in our lives.

6. WRAP UP

When our feet are fitted with the readiness that comes from the gospel of peace, we're prepared to stand—even when Satan's hellfire makes the ground hot. We're also prepared to move—to go wherever God wants us to go, walking in His marvelous light as the Spirit leads us.

7. FINAL LESSON

There is nothing Satan can do to destroy the peace we have with God through Jesus Christ.

8. PERSONAL REVIEW QUESTIONS

Circle T (true) or F (false)

1. T F The "good news of peace" refers to the day to come when all the nations of the world are at peace.

2. T F Because of Jesus' death on the cross, we can now have peace with God.

3. T F The only thing that can separate a Christian from God's love is Satan.

4. T F We should always be prepared to tell others about what Jesus has done for us.

5. T F When God told Abraham to leave his home, Abraham waited for more explicit instructions before setting out.

6. T F God promises to guide our steps.

7. T F God guides us through the scriptures and through the leading of His Holy Spirit.

8. T F There's no way to tell whether or not a person is living a life that is led by the Spirit.

9. T F If we want to walk in the light, we should imitate our pastor.

10. T F If we follow Jesus, we will never walk in darkness.

9. MEMORY VERSE

Ephesians 6:10-15 (Memorize, then write it on these lines.)

_____

_____

_____

_____

_____

_____

_____

_____

_____

_____

10. PRACTICAL EXERCISE

This week ask God to send one person into your life who needs Jesus Christ—then share your knowledge and faith with that person.

HOW DID THE PERSON RESPOND?

_____

_____

_____

TRUE OR FALSE ANSWERS:

1-F, 2-T, 3-F, 4-T, 5-F, 6-T, 7-T, 8-F, 9-F, 10-T.

Lesson 7
The Shield of Faith
VIDEO REFERENCE: #7

I. Introduction

The warriors of ancient Rome had two kinds of shields. The first, called a buckler, was small and round and was usually strapped to the soldier's arm. In hand-to-hand combat, he could use the buckler to fend off the blows of his enemy while swinging a short sword with his other hand.

The second type shield was much larger—called a battle shield. Made to fit his specific measurements, the battle shield provided the soldier with head-to-foot protection. If he had his shield up, the stones and flaming arrows flung by the enemy could not harm him.

It is this second type shield that Paul has in mind when he talks about the next piece of armor we need to put on in spiritual warfare.

2. The Shield of Faith

AFTER WE PUT ON THE SHOES OF READINESS, WHAT IS THE NEXT PIECE OF ARMOR PAUL TELLS US TO TAKE UP? (Ephesians 6:16)

_____

Paul begins this verse with, "In addition to all this. . . ." Another translation would be, "Above all. . . ." Above all, we are to take up the shield of faith. This does not mean that the shield is more important than any other piece of armor. Paul was not speaking of importance, but of position. The shield of faith is to be *over us*, protecting us from the attack of the enemy.

But what is faith? If the shield of faith is supposed to be over us, covering us from head to toe, it is crucial to the spiritual battle we are waging that we know what faith means.

WHAT IS THE DEFINITION OF FAITH GIVEN IN HEBREWS 11:1?

_____

_____

TO COME TO GOD, WHAT TWO THINGS MUST WE BELIEVE? (Hebrews 11:6)

1. _____

2. _____

If we believe God exists even though we can't physically see Him, then we are "certain of what we do not see." If we believe God rewards those who seek Him, then we can be "sure of what we hope for."

Simplified, the definition of faith is this: believing God. Believing what He says in the Bible. Believing what He whispers in our hearts, either privately or through one of His messengers. God has said it—so it is true.

3. THE IMPORTANCE OF FAITH

WITHOUT _____*faith*_____, IT IS IMPOSSIBLE TO PLEASE GOD. (Hebrews 11:6).

The Bible is constantly talking about faith. That's because faith is important to God. When people believe God, God Himself is pleased.

When Moses led the people of Israel out of Egypt, God promised to guide and protect them and bring them to a land "flowing with milk and honey." But along the 40-year journey, the people began to doubt God. They rebelled against God's chosen leader, Moses. Paul refers to this dark period of Jewish history in Hebrews 3:7-19.

WHAT DID THE ISRAELITES DO DURING THE REBELLION THAT ANGERED GOD? (Hebrews 3:8)

_____

WHY WERE THE ISRAELITES NOT ALLOWED TO ENTER THE PROMISED LAND?(Hebrews 3:19)

_____

God wanted to bless His people, but He could not because of their unbelief. God still wants to bless His people. But without faith, we miss His blessing.

4. THE POWER OF FAITH

When we believe God, things happen. Faith in God and in His Son, Jesus Christ, is the most powerful force available to man.

WHAT HEALED THE SICK WOMAN? (Matthew 9:20-22)

_____ the power in Jesus' cloak

_____ the power of positive thinking

_____ her faith in Jesus

HOW WAS THE CENTURION'S SERVANT HEALED? (Matthew 8:5-13)

_____ Jesus went to him and healed him

_____ The centurion returned to him and laid hands on him in Jesus' name

_____ The centurion believed the word of Jesus

HOW DO WE MOVE THE MOUNTAINS IN OUR LIVES? (Mark 11:22-23)

_____

_____

WHAT IS THE KEY ELEMENT IN RECEIVING ANSWERS TO OUR PRAYERS? (Mark 11:24)

_____

_____

WHAT DOES JESUS SAY WE WILL BE ABLE TO DO IF WE HAVE FAITH IN HIM? (John 14:12)

_____

_____

What did Jesus do while He was on earth? He healed the sick. He cast out demons. He raised the dead. He overcame every temptation and won the victory over Satan. We, too, can do these things—and, He says, even greater things through the power of the Holy Spirit—if we have faith in Him.

But what if our faith is shaky? What if we want to believe, but we're having trouble doing it? We're not alone.

WHAT DID THE APOSTLES ASK JESUS TO DO? (Luke 17:5)

_____"Increase our faith"_____

HOW MUCH FAITH DID JESUS SAY WAS NECESSARY TO UPROOT THE MULBERRY TREE? (Luke 17:6)

_____faith as a mustard seed =_____

Mk 4:26 – 29

Read Mark 9:14-27.

WHAT DID JESUS SAY WAS POSSIBLE IF WE BELIEVE? (Mark 9:23)

All things

WHAT WAS THE FATHER'S SOMEWHAT CONTRADICTORY RESPONSE? (Mark 9:24)

I believe, help my unbelief.

WHAT DID JESUS DO? (Mark 9:25)

He answered the fathers request

Most of us can identify with this father. He believed a little—and he wanted to believe more. Apparently, he believed Jesus enough for a great miracle to occur. It was a lesson that undoubtedly increased his faith—for more faith always comes when we exercise the faith we have.

Notice that Jesus did not rebuke the father for admitting he needed more faith. That's a request God loves to answer.

ACCORDING TO HEBREWS 12:2, WHERE DOES OUR FAITH ORIGINATE?

w/ Jesus

WHO WILL PERFECT OUR FAITH? (Hebrews 12:2)

Jesus

5. EXTINGUISHING THE FLAMING ARROWS

No one is more aware of the power of faith than Satan. That's why he tries to attack our faith at every turn.

WHAT WAS SATAN'S QUESTION TO EVE IN THE GARDEN OF EDEN? (Genesis 3:1)

Did God really say ——— ?

God told Adam and Eve they would die if they ate from the tree of the knowledge of good and evil.

WHAT DID SATAN SAY ABOUT THAT? (Genesis 3:4)

_____ God was right and they should believe Him.

_____ God had lied and they should not believe Him.

ADAM AND EVE CHOSE TO BELIEVE: (Genesis 3:6)

_____ God

_____ Satan

Every temptation is, very simply, an opportunity to choose whom we will believe—Satan or God. From the beginning of history, Satan has tried to cause men and women to doubt God. Thoughts and temptations, doubts and fears—these are Satan's "flaming arrows." If allowed to penetrate, their poison tips inject increasingly lethal doses of unbelief into our very souls. That's why we have the shield of faith. It alone can deflect the fiery darts.

But faith must be applied to be effective.

WHERE DOES PAUL SAY THE WORD OF FAITH IS? (Romans 10:8)

_____ *in our mouth* _____

_____

WHAT TWO FACTORS ARE INVOLVED IN OUR SALVATION? (Romans 10:9-10)

1. _____ *heart* _____

2. _____ *mouth* _____

Believing in our hearts is not enough. We have to speak the word of faith.

HOW DO WE OVERCOME SATAN? (Revelation 12:11)

1. _____ *By the blood of the Lamb* _____

2. _____ *By the word of testimony* _____
        Not loving our lives unto death

We believe God, we speak our faith, and Satan is defeated. That means when the devil whispers lies to us, when he plants thoughts in our minds that contradict what we know God has said, we hold up our shield and shout, "Not so, Satan. I believe God." That's how Jesus had victory in his battle with Satan in the wilderness. And that's how we have victory, too.

6. FIGHT THE GOOD FIGHT

WHAT DO THE FOLLOWING SCRIPTURES TELL US ABOUT OUR FAITH?

II Corinthians 1:24 _____

_____

I Peter 1:5 _____

_____

I Peter 5:8-9 _____

_____

I John 5:4 _____

_____

WHAT DOES PAUL ENCOURAGE US TO DO IN I TIMOTHY 6:12?

_____

WHAT WARNING DOES HE GIVE IN HEBREWS 3:12?

_____

_____

HOW CAN WE KEEP EACH OTHER FROM FALLING INTO UNBELIEF?
(Hebrews 3:13)

_____

_____

WHY DID PAUL EXPECT TO BE AWARDED THE CROWN OF
RIGHTEOUSNESS? (II Timothy 4:7-8)

_____

_____

7. WRAP UP

Our faith is the shield that gives us full coverage against all of Satan's attacks. When we believe God—when we believe what He says in the Bible and what He speaks to our hearts—we unleash not only great blessing but also the power to be victorious against every one of Satan's schemes.

8. FINAL LESSON

Every temptation is an opportunity to believe God—and defeat Satan.

9. PERSONAL REVIEW QUESTIONS

Circle T (true) or F (false)

1. T F It is impossible to believe in something we cannot see.

2. T F God is pleased when we put our faith in Him.

3. T F God allowed the Israelites to enter the Promised Land, even though they had not believed Him.

4. T F Adam and Eve fell because they believed Satan rather than God.

5.   T   F   Miracles happen when we put our faith in Jesus.

6.   T   F   If we believe strongly enough in ourselves, we can move mountains.

7.   T   F   Jesus was angry when the father of the demon-possessed boy asked Him to help him believe.

8.   T   F   It is impossible to increase your faith.

9.   T   F   To defeat Satan, we must not simply believe; we must speak our faith.

10.   T   F   Once we put our faith in God, we do not have to worry about falling into unbelief.

10. MEMORY VERSE

Ephesians 6:10-16 (Memorize, then write it on these lines.)

_____

_____

_____

_____

_____

_____

_____

_____

_____

_____

11. PRACTICAL EXERCISE

This week speak the "word of faith" when you are attacked by Satan. Note at least one instance when this happens:

_____

_____

_____

_____

TRUE OR FALSE ANSWERS:

1-F, 2-T, 3-F, 4-T, 5-T, 6-F, 7-F, 8-F, 9-T, 10-F

NOTES

LESSON 8
THE HELMET OF SALVATION
VIDEO REFERENCE: #8

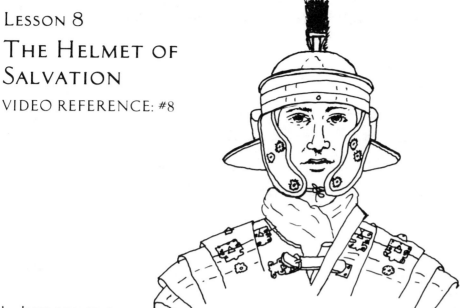

1. INTRODUCTION

When a Roman warrior dressed for battle, the last piece of armor he put on was the helmet. It was a critical element for an effective defense. The helmet protected the soldier from oncoming arrows; but even more importantly, it protected him from the death blow of his opponent's broadsword. The broadsword was massive and heavy, usually three to four feet long. A warrior would hold it with two hands, swing it over his head and bring it down upon the head of his enemy. The crushing blow was debilitating—or fatal.

It was to fend off an attack from Satan's "broadsword" that the Ephesians were encouraged to put on the next piece of spiritual armor.

2. THE HELMET OF SALVATION

What is the final piece of armor Paul tells us to put on before taking up our sword? (Ephesians 6:17)

_____

In the language of the Old Testament, the word "salvation" means "deliverance." In fact, "salvation" and "deliverance" are interchangeable terms. Where some translations of the Bible read "God saves," others read "God delivers," and vice versa.

But what does it mean to be delivered?

Early in His ministry, Jesus visited the synagogue in His hometown of Nazareth. During the service He stood up and quoted from a prophetic passage in the Old Testament, Isaiah 61:1-2, telling His listeners that He was the prophecy's fulfillment.

READ LUKE 4:14-21. WHAT SIX THINGS DID JESUS SAY HE HAD COME TO DO? (Luke 4:18-19)

1. _____

2. _____

3. _____

4. _____

5. _____

6. _____

Paul uses another term for "the year of the Lord's favor" in II Corinthians 6:2.

WHAT IS IT? _____

Salvation means to be *set free*. Jesus was talking about salvation that day in the synagogue. He came to set people free—to unleash the poor from the chains of poverty, to free the prisoners, to deliver the blind from their infirmity, to release the oppressed. When we are saved we are set free from whatever has us bound up—whether it be habits, oppression, tradition, sickness, sin, fear, or circumstances.

Usually, when we say we've "been saved," we mean we've been set free from the penalty of our sins. The Bible says that "the wages of sin is death." However, Jesus' death on the cross paid that price for each one of us. When we put our faith in Jesus, we're delivered from condemnation—instantly and eternally. That's a salvation Satan can never take from us, and it is our greatest defense against his attacks. However, once we become Christians, there are still things from which we must be set free. It is to people who were already Christians—those who were already "saved"—that Paul wrote, "Take the helmet of salvation. . . ."

3. SET FREE FROM AFFLICTION

Satan and his demons attack Christians in three ways. The first of these is through affliction—making us sick or creating terrible circumstances that afflict and debilitate us. But God has given us the helmet of salvation—and we can trust Him to set us free from whatever affliction the devil lays upon us.

When the people of Israel first left the bondage of Egypt under the leadership of Moses, they were pursued by an angry Egyptian army. The Israelites fled to the edge of the Red Sea and were trapped there as the Egyptian troops approached. They railed against Moses, saying, "Why did you bring us out here to die? We'd have been better off staying in Egypt as slaves!"

How did Moses answer the people? (Exodus 14:13)

_____

_____

Explain how God delivered the Israelites. (Exodus 14:15-31)

_____

_____

_____

A major theme throughout the Psalms is God's deliverance of David and the people of Israel.

In Psalm 34, what does David say God saved him from?

1. (Psalm 34:4) _____

2. (Psalm 34:6) _____

Whom is the Lord close to? (Psalm 34:18) _____

Whom does God save? (Psalm 34:18) _____

In the New Testament, Paul, too, talks about God's deliverance.

How difficult were Paul's circumstances in the province of Asia? (II Corinthians 1:8-9)

_____

_____

_____

Who delivered him? (II Corinthians 1:10)

_____

WHAT DID PAUL EXPECT GOD TO CONTINUE TO DO? (II Corinthians 1:10)

_____

WHAT THINGS SHOULD A CHRISTIAN BE ANXIOUS ABOUT? (Philippians 4:6)

_____

WHAT SHOULD WE DO WHEN WE BEGIN TO FEEL ANXIOUS? (Philippians 4:6)

_____

_____

WHAT CAN WE EXPECT TO HAPPEN WHEN WE DO THIS? (Philippians 4:7)

_____

_____

HOW WAS PAUL ABLE TO OVERCOME HIS CIRCUMSTANCES? (Philippians 4:13)

_____

Circumstances, fear, trouble, brokenheartedness, illness—these things do not have to control the lives of Christians who put on the helmet of salvation. We need only to call on the Lord, have faith in his deliverance, and move through our circumstances in the strength of Jesus.

4. SET FREE FROM BONDAGE

The second way demons attack Christians is through bondage—habits, sin, tradition, resistance to change. Bondages are those things which control us and motivate our behavior—when we ought to be led by the Spirit of God.

When we become Christians, we are freed from the penalty of our sins. But that does not mean our struggle with sin is over.

DESCRIBE PAUL'S STRUGGLE IN ROMANS 7:15-23.

_____

_____

_____

_____

Paul is talking about bondage—about being controlled by the power of sin. He could be describing a sinful habit or an immoral lifestyle. But basically he's talking about something inside of him that *likes* to sin—that keeps on sinning, even though he knows it's not the right thing to do. If we're honest, most of us can identify with him in some areas of our lives.

WHAT DOES JESUS SET US FREE FROM? (Romans 8:2)

_____

_____

The scripture teaches that when Jesus died on the cross, we died with Him. It was *our* death—the death that we deserved because of our sins—that He died on Calvary.

WHAT HAPPENED TO OUR OLD, SINFUL NATURES? (Romans 6:6)

_____

WE NEED TO THINK OF OURSELVES AS: (Romans 6:11)

1. Dead to _____

2. Alive to _____

WHAT SHOULD WE SET OUR MINDS ON? (Romans 8:5-6)

_____

When we forget to put on the helmet of salvation—when we let down our guard and forget to set our minds daily on the things of the Spirit—we give the devil a foothold in our lives. Satan loves to put us into bondage and will take advantage of whatever inroad we give him.

Sometimes that inroad can be "religious." A demon can as effectively debilitate a believer by binding him with religious tradition and a resistance to change as by causing him to fail morally.

That was the problem with the fledgling church in Galatia. Jewish tradition taught that all baby boys were to be circumcised as a sign of Israel's covenant with God. Jesus' death and resurrection ushered in a New Covenant, however, that became available to Jew and Gentile alike. Still, the Galatian Christians thought they needed to be circumcised—to follow religious tradition—in order to be right with God.

TO WHAT DID PAUL COMPARE THE RELIGIOUS TRADITION? (Galatians 5:1)

_____

WHAT DID HE TELL THE GALATIANS TO DO? (Galatians 5:1)

_____

WHAT WARNING DID PAUL GIVE TO THE COLOSSIAN CHURCH? (Colossians 2:8)

_____

_____

_____

WHAT DID JESUS SAY WAS THE PROBLEM WITH THE PHARISEES? (Mark 7:6)

_____

_____

Traditions are not wrong in and of themselves. However, being a Christian is not a matter of following a set of religious traditions—it's a matter of being led by the Spirit of God. If the Spirit is not present in it, we must be willing to leave a tradition behind in order to follow the Spirit. We must be willing to go where He goes, to change our course—and our minds—when necessary.

The apostle Peter's resistance to change almost kept the non-Jewish world from hearing the gospel. God had to convince Peter through a dream that the New Convenant was open to Gentiles, too.

READ ACTS 10:1-11:18. WHAT WAS PETER'S BUILT-IN RESISTANCE TO VISITING THE HOUSE OF CORNELIUS? (Acts 10:28)

_____

WHAT HAD GOD TAUGHT HIM THAT CONVINCED HIM TO GO ANYWAY?
(Acts 10:34)

_____

_____

WHAT WAS THE RESULT OF PETER'S WILLINGNESS TO CHANGE? (Acts 11:18)

_____

_____

5. SET FREE FROM TEMPTATION

The third way Satan and his demons attack Christians is through temptation. The world is full of pleasures and enticements that can draw us away from God. But the Bible tells us not to be conformed to this world—not to think like it, not to be influenced by it.

WHAT WARNING DOES JOHN GIVE IN 1 JOHN 2:15?

_____

_____

_____

WHAT IS THE DIFFERENCE BETWEEN THE THINGS OF THE WORLD AND THE THINGS OF GOD? (I John 2:17)

_____

_____

WHAT DOES PAUL TELL US TO DO IN ROMANS 12:2?

_____

_____

_____

_____

Renewing our minds is critical if we are going to win in spiritual warfare. We live in a world of thoughts. Many of them are evil, immoral. They come into our minds through our senses: our eyes, our ears, our noses, and our mouths. But the helmet of salvation covers all these openings, protecting us from evil and allowing us to think only God-thoughts.

ACCORDING TO THE FOLLOWING SCRIPTURES, HOW DO WE "RENEW OUR MINDS"?

Psalm 1:1-2 _____

_____

_____

Matthew 22:37 _____

_____

II Corinthians 10:5 _____

_____

_____

Philippians 4:8 _____

_____

_____

_____

Colossians 3:2 _____

_____

We put on the helmet of salvation by letting the Holy Spirit renew our minds daily. Then we are prepared to triumph over every temptation Satan and his demons deploy.

WHAT PROMISES ARE CONTAINED IN THE FOLLOWING SCRIPTURES?

I Corinthians 10:13 _____

_____

_____

_____

Hebrews 2:18 _____

_____

6. WRAP UP

Jesus came to set us free—not only from the penalty of our sins, but also from the afflictions, bondages, and temptations Satan and his demons use to attack and debilitate us. When we put on the helmet of salvation, we remind ourselves—and tell the forces of evil—that we are trusting God to deliver us. Then we let the Holy Spirit renew our minds. When our minds are set on God, the helmet of salvation keeps Satan locked out.

7. FINAL LESSON

"But since we belong to the day, let us be self-controlled, putting on. . . the hope of salvation as a helmet. For God did not appoint us to suffer wrath but to receive salvation through our Lord Jesus Christ" (I Thessalonians 5:8-9).

8. PERSONAL REVIEW QUESTIONS

Circle T (true) or F (false)

1. T F Salvation means to be "set free."

2. T F Once a Christian is saved from the penalty of his sins, he has no further need of deliverance.

3. T F Satan and his demons try to attack us through affliction, bondage, and temptation.

4. T F When we find ourselves in difficult circumstances, it is up to us to get ourselves out.

5. T F We can face anything when we trust Christ to strengthen us.

6. T F We cannot expect to be set free from our ingrained habits or lifestyles because the power of sin is too strong.

7. T F Paul never struggled with sin.

8. T F We must be willing to change—even set aside our religious traditions—in order to follow the Spirit of God.

9. T F We should love the things of this world with all our hearts, souls, and minds.

10. T F God provides a way out of every temptation.

9. MEMORY VERSE

Ephesians 6:10-17 (Memorize, then write it on these lines.)

_____
_____
_____
_____
_____
_____
_____
_____
_____
_____
_____
_____

10. PRACTICAL EXERCISE

LIST TWO SPECIFIC WAYS SATAN HAS IN THE PAST OR IS NOW ATTACKING YOU IN EACH OF THE FOLLOWING THREE AREAS. WHAT HAVE YOU DONE, OR WHAT DO YOU NEED TO DO, TO DEFEAT HIM?

A) AFFLICTION

1. _____
_____

2. _____
_____

B) Bondage

1. _____
   _____

2. _____
   _____

C) Temptation

1. _____
   _____

2. _____
   _____

TRUE OR FALSE ANSWERS:

1-T, 2-F, 3-T, 4-F, 5-T, 6-F, 7-F, 8-T, 9-F, 10-T.

NOTES

LESSON 9
THE SWORD OF THE SPIRIT
VIDEO REFERENCE: #9

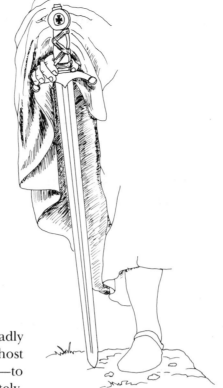

1. INTRODUCTION

The Christian is in a war against a deadly but invisible enemy. Satan and his host of demons have but one purpose—to destroy and kill the believer. Fortunately, the Bible tells us exactly how to fight the enemy—and not only how to hold our own, but to come out victorious: put on the full armor of God.

When preparing for battle, the last weapon the Roman warrior picked up was his sword. He had a short sword and long sword. He could use his short sword for defense, parrying off an attack from the enemy. But primarily he used it for offense, thrusting it at his opponent with the intent to maim or kill. The long sword, on the other hand, was swung. If the soldier was aggressive enough, and the rest of his armor was in place, he could swing his sword and cut a path right through the enemy's lines—without being harmed.

So it is with the Christian's sword.

2. THE CHRISTIAN'S SWORD

WHAT IS THE FINAL WEAPON PAUL TELLS US TO PICK UP? (Ephesians 6:17)

_____

WHAT DOES PAUL SAY THE SWORD IS? (Ephesians 6:17)

_____

The writer of Hebrews also compares the word of God to a sword.

HOW DOES HEBREWS 4:12A DESCRIBE THE WORD OF GOD?

_____

NOTES

WHAT DOES THE WORD OF GOD DO? (Hebrews 4:12)

1. _____

_____

2. _____

ACCORDING TO ISAIAH 55:11, CAN THE WORD OF GOD EVER FAIL TO ACHIEVE ITS PURPOSE?

_____ yes

_____ no

Obviously we are talking about a weapon of great power and effect. But what exactly is the word of God?

Most people equate the "Word of God" with the Bible. There is a strong sense in which the word does represent scripture—although at the time Paul wrote his letter to the Ephesians, the Bible as we know it was not in existence and the scrolls of the Old Testament were kept in synagogues. Still, the Bible has much to say about the importance of the scriptures in spiritual warfare.

According to II Timothy 3:16, the Bible equips the Christian for the work God calls him to do.

IN WHAT FOUR WAYS IS SCRIPTURE USEFUL?

1. _____

2. _____

3. _____

4. _____

WHAT DO THE FOLLOWING PASSAGES HAVE TO SAY ABOUT THE PURPOSE OF THE WRITTEN WORD?

John 20:31 _____

_____

Acts 17:10-12 _____

_____

Romans 10:17 _____

_____

Romans 15:4 _____

_____

II Peter 3:1 _____

_____

WHAT DID JESUS SAY WAS THE ERROR OF THE SADDUCEES? (Mark 12:24)

_____

_____

WHAT ADMONITION DOES PAUL GIVE HIS YOUNG PROTEGE, TIMOTHY, WITH REGARD TO THE WORD OF GOD (TRUTH)? (II Timothy 2:15)

_____

_____

WHAT TWO ADMONITIONS DOES PETER GIVE?

II Peter 3:2 _____

_____

I Peter 3:15 _____

_____

_____

HOW DID JESUS COMBAT SATAN WHEN SATAN TRIED TO TEMPT HIM IN THE WILDERNESS? (Luke 4:4, 8, 12)

_____ He used supernatural power to disarm him

_____ He quoted from scripture

_____ He challenged him to a sword fight

Jesus' sword was the Word of God. We, too, can defeat the enemy by studying the Bible and handling it correctly—answering Satan's accusations and temptations with a scriptural response. Satan cannot stand against God's Word.

3. THE WORD BECAME FLESH

For years men have debated the Bible. Is it the Word of God; does it contain the word of God; or does it merely point you to the One who is the word of God? The answer is: yes—to all three.

The apostle John talked about the Word of God—but he was not referring to the scriptures.

WHERE WAS THE WORD AT THE BEGINNING OF ALL THINGS? (John 1:1-2)

_____

WHAT WAS THE WORD'S ROLE IN CREATION? (John 1:3)

_____

JOHN SAYS "THE WORD BECAME FLESH AND LIVED FOR A WHILE AMONG US." TO WHOM WAS HE REFERRING? (John 1:14-18)

_____

EVEN THOUGH WE HAVE NEVER SEEN GOD, WE CAN KNOW HIM. HOW? (John 1:18)

_____

JESUS IS GOD'S WORD TO US—THE EXPRESSION HE USES TO TELL US WHO HE IS. THE SCRIPTURES TESTIFY ABOUT:

_____ (John 5:39).

THE JEWS STUDIED THE SCRIPTURES. YET JESUS SAID THEY MADE A BASIC MISTAKE. WHAT WAS IT? (John 5:39-40)

_____

THE JEWS KNEW THE WORD OF GOD BUT THEY DIDN'T HAVE THE WORD OF GOD DWELLING INSIDE THEM. WHY? (John 5:38)

_____

WHAT GIVES US LIFE? (John 5:39-40)

_____ bread and water

_____ a knowledge of the scriptures

_____ Jesus

It is important to study the Bible. But in and of themselves, the scriptures have no power to give life—only Jesus does. A knowledge of the Bible, without a personal knowledge of the One to whom it testifies—Jesus Christ—is dry, dead legalism.

4. Power in the Blood

The Roman sword had a peculiar feature—a groove called a "blood channel" forged into both sides of the blade. When the sword was thrust into a human body, often the suction that formed kept the warrior from withdrawing the blade. The blood channel broke that suction so the sword could be withdrawn.

Blood is an unavoidable factor in battle. The shedding of blood means death for the victim—and life for the victor. But in spiritual warfare, that blood has already been shed.

WHAT DID JOHN THE BAPTIST CALL JESUS? (John 1:29)

_____

HOW DID PETER REFER TO JESUS? (I Peter 1:19)

_____

God had told the Jews the only way they could have their sins forgiven was by blood sacrifice. Each year a perfect lamb was killed in the temple— its blood shed as a symbol of atonement. But when the Messiah came, all that changed. Jesus was sacrificed, once for all. During Jesus' last supper with His disciples before He was crucified, He made reference to His own blood.

WHAT DID HE SAY? (Matthew 26:28)

_____

WHAT HAS THE SHED BLOOD OF JESUS DONE FOR US?

Romans 5:9_____

_____

Ephesians 1:7 _____

_____

Colossians 1:19-20 _____

I John 1:7 _____

_____

_____

The blood is at the heart of everything we believe. In spiritual warfare it is mandatory that we fight the enemy with the blood of Jesus. If our sword does not have a blood channel, it is useless.

HOW IS SATAN DEFEATED? (Revelation 12:11)

_____

_____

Satan is defeated by the blood of Jesus and by the word of our testimony that we are "under the blood." Although we are constantly under attack, we are protected from demon harm because of the blood of Jesus.

5. THE LIVING WORD

The sword of the Spirit, Paul says, is the word of God. In Greek there are two words for the one translated into English as "word." The first is *logos*, which has come to mean the written word. The other is *rhema*. This is the one Paul uses to describe the Christian's sword. It means a word, spoken by God, alive in our hearts. When Paul talks about the Christian's sword, he is not talking about the Bible per se—he is talking about the Living Word, the Spirit who lives within us. It is the Spirit who gives us power to defeat the enemy.

JESUS SAID THAT "STREAMS OF LIVING WATER" WOULD FLOW FROM THOSE WHO BELIEVE IN HIM. TO WHAT WAS HE REFERRING? (John 7:37-39)

_____

WHO WAS TO RECEIVE THE HOLY SPIRIT? (John 7:39)

_____

WHAT WAS THE PROMISE JESUS REPEATED IN JOHN 14:16, 14:26 AND 16:7?

_____

After His resurrection, Jesus appeared to His disciples and commanded them to wait in Jerusalem for the gift He had talked about—God's promise of the Holy Spirit.

WHAT DID JESUS SAY WOULD HAPPEN TO THE DISCIPLES? (Acts 1:5)

_____

WHAT WOULD THEY RECEIVE WHEN THE HOLY SPIRIT CAME UPON THEM? (Acts 1:8)

_____

WHAT HAPPENED TO THE DISCIPLES ON THE DAY OF PENTECOST? (Acts 2:1-4)

_____

_____

Jesus knew the disciples needed the power of the Holy Spirit before they were sent out into the world. The Holy Spirit changed their lives. The small band of frightened, discouraged believers, huddled in that upper room, suddenly became energized— empowered to preach the gospel with authority, heal the sick, cast out demons, and conquer Satan. If we want to be victorious in spiritual warfare, we need that power, too.

WHAT DO WE NEED TO DO TO RECEIVE THE HOLY SPIRIT? (Luke 11:13)

_____

HOW DO WE RECEIVE THE PROMISE OF THE HOLY SPIRIT? (Galatians 3:14)

_____

LOOK UP THE FOLLOWING SCRIPTURES: JOHN 14:16-17; I CORINTHIANS 3:16; GALATIANS 4:6. WHERE DOES THE SPIRIT RESIDE?

_____

According to the following scriptures, what are some of the things the Spirit does in us and for us?

Luke 12:11-12 _____

John 14:26 _____

_____

Romans 8:11 _____

Romans 8:26 _____

_____

I Corinthians 2:12 _____

_____

What does it mean to pick up the sword of the Spirit? It means being filled with the Spirit of God.

6. WRAP UP

The Christian's one weapon that is offensive as well as defensive is the sword of the Spirit, which is the word of God. The word refers to scripture, which, as Jesus demonstrated during His temptations in the wilderness, is an effective defense against Satan's attacks. It also refers to Jesus, through whose blood we have received the remission of our sins. But finally, the word of God refers to the Living Word—the Holy Spirit living in us, Who gives us power to be victorious in spiritual warfare.

7. FINAL LESSON

Even though we may be clothed in the full armor of God and live protected lives, we'll never have the power Jesus gave His disciples—the power to overcome demons and conquer Satan, the power to have personal victory over the problems in our lives—unless we are filled with the Holy Spirit.

8. PERSONAL REVIEW QUESTIONS

Circle T (true) or F (false)

1. T   F   When Paul talked about the word of God, he meant the Bible as we know it today.

2. T   F   Knowledge of the scriptures is important in spiritual warfare.

3. T   F   Jesus used supernatural power to defeat Satan in the wilderness.

4. T   F   The Word became flesh and lived for a while among us.

5. T   F   Jesus was called the "Lamb of God" because of His meek and gentle nature.

6. T   F   Satan is defeated by the blood of the Lamb and the word of our testimony.

7. T   F   When the disciples received the Holy Spirit, they were surprised because Jesus had never mentioned anything about it.

8. T   F   The disciples received power when the Holy Spirit came upon them.

9. T   F   If we ask God, He will give us the Holy Spirit.

10. T   F   Picking up the sword of the Spirit means being filled with the Spirit of God.

9. MEMORY VERSE

Ephesians 6:10-18 (Memorize, then write it on these lines.)

_____
_____
_____
_____
_____
_____
_____
_____
_____
_____
_____
_____
_____
_____
_____
_____

10. PRACTICAL EXERCISE

FIND TWO VERSES OF SCRIPTURE THAT YOU CAN USE TO FIGHT SATAN AS HE ATTACKS YOU IN YOUR AREAS OF WEAKNESS. BE PREPARED TO DESCRIBE HOW THESE VERSES DEFEATED THE ENEMY WHEN YOU USED THEM.

Verse 1: _____
_____
_____

Verse 2: _____
_____
_____

TRUE OR FALSE ANSWERS:

1-F, 2-T, 3-F, 4-T, 5-F, 6-T, 7-F, 8-T, 9-T, 10-T

LESSON 10

PRAYING IN THE SPIRIT

VIDEO REFERENCE: #10

1. INTRODUCTION

You and I are in the midst of a spiritual battle. Satan and his host of demons—the rulers, the authorities, the powers and spiritual forces of evil in the heavenly realms—are engaged in an invisible war—and we are the targets. Satan wants to kill, steal from and destroy the children of God. But God has not left us defenseless. In fact, He has provided everything we need to be victorious against the enemy.

Not only do we have a powerful force of allies—the angels—fighting with us and for us, we have spiritual armor that is capable of giving us head-to-toe protection from demon attack. We also have a weapon—the sword of the Spirit—designed to deal the enemy his death blow.

It would seem that the Christian's preparation is complete. We now know how to arm ourselves effectively for victory in spiritual warfare. Yet Paul, in his letter to the Ephesians, says there is one more thing we must do.

2. THE IMPORTANCE OF PRAYER

AFTER WE HAVE PUT ON OUR SPIRITUAL ARMOR, WHAT DOES PAUL SAY WE MUST DO? (Ephesians 6:18)

_____

_____

There are more commands in the Bible to pray than to do anything else. Why? Prayer is the lubrication that keeps our spiritual armor working. Without it we become clanking legalists—our joints eventually rusting together, immobilizing us. We have the Word. We're protected by God's armor. But we can't move. We can't advance. We can't fight.

What is prayer? Here is a simple definition: Prayer is talking to God. Prayer is God talking to us.

The Bible says Jesus often withdrew to pray. He was constantly aware of the warfare raging in the unseen spiritual world—and knew that prayer was the only way to win that war.

READ MARK 1:35; LUKE 5:16; LUKE 6:12-16. ARE THE FOLLOWING STATEMENTS TRUE OR FALSE?

Circle T (true) or F (false)

T   F   Jesus sometimes woke early in the morning to pray.

T   F   Jesus sometimes prayed all night long.

T   F   Jesus sought solitude in order to pray.

T   F   Jesus' concern for the multitudes who needed His ministry led Him to sometimes skip His prayer time.

T   F   After Jesus chose His twelve apostles, He prayed all night for God's blessing on His decision.

Prayer was important to Jesus. Paul says it must also be important to us.

ACCORDING TO EPHESIANS 6:18:
ON WHAT OCCASIONS SHOULD WE PRAY?

_____

_____

WHAT KINDS OF PRAYERS AND REQUESTS SHOULD WE MAKE?

_____

_____

HOW OFTEN SHOULD WE PRAY FOR OTHER CHRISTIANS?

_____

3. PRAYING ALWAYS

Paul tells us to pray always. That doesn't mean our lips are moving all the time. Paul is talking about an attitude of prayer—a God-conciousness in which we live every moment with an awareness of God's presence.

WHEN DID JESUS SAY HE WOULD BE WITH US? (Matthew 28:20)

_____

_____

HOW CLOSE IS JESUS TO US? (John 14:20)

_____

WITH WHOM DO WE HAVE FELLOWSHIP AS CHRISTIANS? (I John 1:3)

_____

_____

When we live in daily awareness of our constant fellowship with God, it becomes natural to talk to Him about everything that touches us throughout the day.

WHAT DO THE FOLLOWING SCRIPTURES TELL US ABOUT HOW AND WHEN TO PRAY?

Romans 12:12 _____

Philippians 4:6_____

_____

Colossians 4:2 _____

_____

I Thessalonians 5:17 _____

4. EXPECTING GOD TO ANSWER

Talking to God is just half of what prayer is about. The other half is listening for what God has to say to us. When we pray, we can expect God to answer.

WHY DOES GOD ANSWER OUR PRAYERS?

1. (John 14:13-14) _____

_____

2. (John 16:24) _____

WHAT DO THE FOLLOWING SCRIPTURES PROMISE US ABOUT ANSWERED PRAYER? NOTE ANY CONDITIONS GIVEN FOR GOD'S RESPONSE.

Matthew 18:19-20 _____

_____

_____

Mark 11:22-24 _____

_____

_____

Luke 11:9-13 _____

_____

_____

_____

John 15:7 _____

_____

James 5:16 _____

_____

_____

I John 5:14-15 _____

_____

_____

ACCORDING TO JAMES, WHY DO WE SOMETIMES LACK WHAT WE NEED? (James 4:2)

_____

_____

WHY DOES GOD NOT ANSWER WHEN WE ASK SOMETHING OF HIM? (James 4:3)

_____

_____

God delights in answering our prayers. But He is not a puppet on a prayer string. He is our Father. In His infinite wisdom, He sometimes does not answer the way we think He should—but in the way He knows is best for us and for His glory.

The apostle Paul was plagued by an unspecified discomfort or disability— a "thorn in the flesh"—which he prayed God would take away.

HOW MANY TIMES DID PAUL PLEAD WITH GOD TO REMOVE THE "THORN"? (II Corinthians 12:8)

_____

WHAT WAS GOD'S RESPONSE? (II Corinthians 12:9)

_____

_____

_____

God responded, but in a different way than Paul had asked—a way that taught Paul how to draw his strength from the Lord.

Jesus, when the time of His death was drawing near, prayed that the Father would take away His "cup"—that He would not have to go to the cross as the means of fulfilling God's plan for the redemption of mankind.

HOW MANY TIMES DID JESUS ASK THE FATHER TO TAKE AWAY HIS "CUP"? (Matthew 26:39-44) _____

WHAT WAS JESUS' ATTITUDE IN MAKING THIS REQUEST? (Matthew 26:42)

_____

Praise God that He sometimes tells us "No"! That was His response to Jesus that night in the Garden. The Son of God was just as submitted to that answer as to any other the Father might have given. As a result, the Lamb of God was sacrificed once for all, and we have forgiveness for our sins.

Sometimes the answer to our prayers is delayed. Occasionally, that is for our good, as God teaches us to wait for His timing. But the delay may also be because of demon interference.

RECALLING BACK TO LESSON 2, WHY WAS THE ANSWER TO DANIEL'S PRAYER DELAYED? (Daniel 10:12-13)

_____

_____

Satan does not want our prayers answered! He wants to destroy our faith by convincing us that God does not hear us and will not answer us. We need to stand on God's promises and place ourselves in a position to receive His answer when we pray. Then we need to be submitted to whatever that answer is, trusting Him to know what is best for us and for His kingdom.

5. HOW TO PRAY

Prayer is conversation with God. It is not a formula. It is not a posture to get in, or certain words to be repeated. It is simply the created talking with the Creator—the child of God talking with His Father.

There are four guidelines, however, that can be helpful when we pray.

1. When possible, *pray out loud*. Silent prayer is just as much prayer as vocal prayer. But when we vocalize something, we indicate we're sincere—that we really believe it. It does us good to pray out loud.

2. *Pray with a notebook in hand.* This way we can write down whatever God speaks back to us—those impressions that come to us from the Holy Spirit within us as we wait quietly before Him. Anything God says is worth writing down—and remembering.

3. *Pray in your native language.*

4. *Pray in the spirit.*

ACCORDING TO 1 CORINTHIANS 14:15, WITH WHAT TWO THINGS SHOULD WE PRAY?

1. _____

2. _____

Praying with your mind or with your understanding means to pray in your native language—your mother tongue. Praying with the spirit, however, is what Paul calls elsewhere "praying in tongues"—using a prayer language that is unintelligible to anyone but God. Not all Spirit-filled Christians use their prayer language. Some pray in the spirit with "groans that words cannot express"—and do it silently. However, if we are praying vocally in the spirit, it will be with a prayer language.

WHO UNDERSTANDS US WHEN WE PRAY IN TONGUES? (I Corinthians 14:2)

_____

HOW DOES THE HOLY SPIRIT HELP US WHEN WE PRAY IN THE SPIRIT? (Romans 8:26)

_____

_____

_____

ARE THE FOLLOWING STATEMENTS TRUE OR FALSE? (Romans 8:26-27)

T   F   We cannot pray unless we know exactly how to pray for a person or situation.

T   F   When we cannot find the words to express ourselves, we must stop praying.

T   F   When we pray in the spirit, the Holy Spirit intercedes for us.

T   F   When we pray in the spirit, we can be sure we are praying in accordance with God's will.

Praying in the spirit pushes back the darkness. When we pray in the spirit we take authority over the things that afflict us—and over things that afflict others. Prayer drives back the demons and gives power to the angels who then go to work fighting our battles in the heavenly realms.

6. BEING ALERT IN PRAYER

Paul tells us in Ephesians 6:18 to "be alert" and pray.

WHAT DOES THE APOSTLE PETER SAY IN I PETER 4:7?

_____

_____

Christians are not supposed to turn their minds off when they accept the Lord. Rather, they are supposed to turn them on.In order to pray effectively, we need to be clear-minded and alert. We need to be aware of the issues of the day and alert to the spiritual forces at war behind those issues. We need to be sensitive to the needs of fellow Christians and the other people around us. We need to be aware of our own needs and alert to the activity of Satan—and the Holy Spirit—in our lives.

Jesus gave us an example of an effective prayer in Matthew 6:9-13. We often call it the "Lord's Prayer." For each verse, note the general topic Jesus says we should pray about and give a more specific example from your own life.

Matthew 6:10 _____

_____

_____

Matthew 6:11 _____

_____

_____

Matthew 6:12 _____

_____

_____

Matthew 6:13 _____

_____

_____

6. WRAP UP

Prayer is the lubricant that keeps our spiritual armor working. When we talk to God—and He talks to us—spiritual forces are set in motion that help to assure victory in our lives and in our battle against Satan. When we pray in the spirit as well as with our understanding, we literally assault the forces of darkness and drive them into the pit.

7. FINAL LESSON

"More things are wrought by prayer than this world dreams" (Alfred, Lord Tennyson).

8. PERSONAL REVIEW QUESTIONS

Circle T (true) or F (false)

1. T F Prayer is talking to God and God talking to us.

2. T F The Bible is not clear about whether or not Jesus prayed.

3. T F We need to walk in constant awareness of God's presence in our lives.

4. T F We should not expect God to answer our prayers.

5. T F Sometimes the reason we don't have the things we need is because we have not asked God.

6. T F God always gives us exactly what we ask for.

7. T F God never said "No" to Jesus.

8. T F If we do not get an immediate answer to our prayers, we should give up.

9. T F It is useless to pray in the spirit since no one can understand us.

10. T F When we do not know exactly how to pray about a situation, we can pray in the spirit and be confident that we are praying in accordance with God's will.

9. MEMORY VERSE

Ephesians 6:10-18 (Review and write it on these lines.)

_____

_____

_____

_____

_____

_____

_____

_____

_____

_____

_____

_____

_____

_____

_____

10. PRACTICAL EXERCISE

Each day this week spend five minutes alone, where no one else can hear you, praying out loud. Spend another five minutes with pen and paper, in silence, writing down what God is saying to you. At the end of the week review what He has said in the presence of someone else. Ask them to confirm, adjust or reject what you think God is saying to you.

TRUE OR FALSE ANSWERS:

1-T, 2-F, 3-T, 4-F, 5-T, 6-F, 7-F, 8-F, 9-F, 10-T

NOTES

Information on Ordering

For additional copies of this workbook

or

for the Video Tape Series designed

to be used with the workbook . . .

or

for the other titles in

Jamie Buckingham's Holy Land Series

Ten Miracles of Jesus

Ten Parables of Jesus

Ten Bible People Like Me

Journey to Spiritual Maturity

write or call:

Paraclete Press

P. O. Box 1568

Orleans, MA 02653

Telephone: 1-800-451-5006

or

buy them at your local Christian bookstore.